Developing Critical Thinking and Problem-Solving Abilities

James E. Stice, *Editor*
University of Texas, Austin

NEW DIRECTIONS FOR TEACHING AND LEARNING
KENNETH E. EBLE, *Editor-in-Chief*
University of Utah, Salt Lake City

Number 30, Summer 1987

Paperback sourcebooks in
The Jossey-Bass Higher Education Series

Jossey-Bass Inc., Publishers
San Francisco • London

James E. Stice (ed.).
Developing Critical Thinking and Problem-Solving Abilities.
New Directions for Teaching and Learning, no. 30.
San Francisco: Jossey-Bass, 1987.

New Directions for Teaching and Learning
Kenneth E. Eble, *Editor-in-Chief*

New Directions for Teaching and Learning is published quarterly
by Jossey-Bass Inc., Publishers. Second-class postage paid at
San Francisco, California, and at additional mailing offices.
POSTMASTER: Send address changes to Jossey-Bass Inc.,
Publishers, 433 California Street, San Francisco, California 94104.

Editorial correspondence should be sent to the Editor-in-Chief,
Kenneth E. Eble, Department of English, University of Utah,
Salt Lake City, Utah 84112.

Library of Congress Catalog Card Number LC 85-644763

International Standard Serial Number ISSN 0271-0633

International Standard Book Number ISBN 1-55542-976-9

Cover art by WILLI BAUM

Manufactured in the United States of America

Ordering Information

The paperback sourcebooks listed below are published quarterly and can be ordered either by subscription or single copy.

Subscriptions cost $48.00 per year for institutions, agencies, and libraries. Individuals can subscribe at the special rate of $36.00 per year *if payment is by personal check.* (Note that the full rate of $48.00 applies if payment is by institutional check, even if the subscription is designated for an individual.) Standing orders are accepted.

Single copies are available at $11.95 when payment accompanies order. (California, New Jersey, New York, and Washington, D.C., residents please include appropriate sales tax.) For billed orders, cost per copy is $11.95 plus postage and handling.

Substantial discounts are offered to organizations and individuals wishing to purchase bulk quantities of Jossey-Bass sourcebooks. Please inquire.

Please note that these prices are for the academic year 1986–1987 and are subject to change without notice. Also, some titles may be out of print and therefore not available for sale.

To ensure correct and prompt delivery, all orders must give either the *name of an individual* or an *official purchase order number.* Please submit your order as follows:

Subscriptions: specify series and year subscription is to begin.
Single Copies: specify sourcebook code (such as, TL1) and first two words of title.

Mail orders for United States and Possessions, Latin America, Canada, Japan, Australia, and New Zealand to:
Jossey-Bass Inc., Publishers
433 California Street
San Francisco, California 94104

Mail orders for all other parts of the world to:
Jossey-Bass Limited
28 Banner Street
London EC1Y 8QE

New Directions for Teaching and Learning Series
Kenneth E. Eble, *Editor-in-Chief*

TL1 *Improving Teaching Styles,* Kenneth E. Eble
TL2 *Learning, Cognition, and College Teaching,* Wilbert J. McKeachie
TL3 *Fostering Critical Thinking,* Robert E. Young

TL4   *Learning About Teaching,* John F. Noonan
TL5   *The Administrator's Role in Effective Teaching,* Alan E. Guskin
TL6   *Liberal Learning and Careers,* Charles S. Green III, Richard G. Salem
TL7   *New Perspectives on Teaching and Learning,* Warren Bryan Martin
TL8   *Interdisciplinary Teaching,* Alvin M. White
TL9   *Expanding Learning Through New Communications Technologies,* Christopher K. Knapper
TL10 *Motivating Professors to Teach Effectively,* James L. Bess
TL11 *Practices That Improve Teaching Evaluation,* Grace French-Lazovik
TL12 *Teaching Writing in All Disciplines,* C. Williams Griffin
TL13 *Teaching Values and Ethics in College,* Michael J. Collins
TL14 *Learning in Groups,* Clark Bouton, Russell Y. Garth
TL15 *Revitalizing Teaching Through Faculty Development,* Paul A. Lacey
TL16 *Teaching Minority Students,* James H. Cones III, John F. Noonan, Denise Janha
TL17 *The First Year of College Teaching,* L. Dee Fink
TL18 *Increasing the Teaching Role of Academic Libraries,* Thomas G. Kirk
TL19 *Teaching and Aging,* Chandra M. N. Mehrotra
TL20 *Rejuvenating Introductory Courses,* Karen I. Spear
TL21 *Teaching as Though Students Mattered,* Joseph Katz
TL22 *Strengthening the Teaching Assistant Faculty,* John D. W. Andrews
TL23 *Using Research to Improve Teaching,* Janet C. Donald, Arthur M. Sullivan
TL24 *College-School Collaboration: Appraising the Major Approaches,* William T. Daly
TL25 *Fostering Academic Excellence Through Honors Programs,* Paul G. Friedman, Reva Jenkins-Friedman
TL26 *Communicating in College Classrooms,* Jean M. Civikly
TL27 *Improving Teacher Education,* Eva C. Galambos
TL28 *Distinguished Teachers on Effective Teaching,* Peter G. Beidler
TL29 *Coping with Faculty Stress,* Peter Seldin

Contents

Editor's Notes   1
James E. Stice

1. Teaching Thinking Through Problem Solving   5
Lois Broder Greenfield
This chapter reviews some attempts to determine the skills that make people good problem solvers and some of the methods that have been developed to teach these skills.

2. Tools for Thinking   23
Moshe F. Rubinstein, Iris R. Firstenberg
Problem-solving ability depends on thinking skills and a knowledge base.
Tools for rational thinking are discussed.

3. The Myers-Briggs Type Indicator: A Jungian Model   37
for Problem Solving
Mary H. McCaulley
The Myers-Briggs Type Indicator is explained, and practical applications
of the theory to the teaching of problem solving are described.

4. How Might I Teach Problem Solving?   55
Donald R. Woods
What we know about teaching problem solving is summarized, and
options that can be used to teach it are critiqued.

5. Teaching Analytical Reasoning Through Thinking Aloud   73
Pair Problem Solving
Jack Lochhead, Arthur Whimbey
The thinking aloud pair problem solving procedure is outlined, and read-
ing comprehension exercises and sample student thought process protocols
are presented.

6. Learning How to Think: Being Earnest Is Important, but   93
It's Not Enough
James E. Stice
Students can get through college by memorizing, but they can come to
grief later on. A plea is made for teachers to teach analytical skills on
purpose instead of hoping that students will develop them on their own.

7. Further Reflections: Useful Resources   **101**

James E. Stice

Some of the limitations of the lecture method for teaching analysis are discussed, some thoughts about the relevance of theories of personality type and learning style to the teaching of problem solving are offered, and a short list of resources is given.

Index   **111**

Editor's Notes

A sourcebook published in this series a half-dozen years ago was titled *Fostering Critical Thinking* (Young, 1980). In that volume, professors of English, education, instructional development, and government discussed critical thinking, also known as *problem solving, analytical reasoning,* or simply *analysis.* The authors all concurred on its importance, agreed that it could be taught, and gave well-reasoned arguments, sometimes backed by personal experiences, for including development of critical thinking skills in the objectives of college courses.

This sourcebook differs from the earlier one in that it addresses the problem of teaching problem solving. Most of the authors are engineering or science teachers, and their efforts are slanted toward helping students learn how to analyze problems involving comprehension of a situation, analysis of elements, calculation of necessary quantities, and evaluation of results. The product of the problems is an answer, which may be followed by a decision to take some course of action. The process generalizes, and I feel that it can be used fruitfully in history, philosophy, and psychology—in short, in almost all disciplines.

The contributors to this sourcebook have all been engaged in attempts to improve students' analytical skills for many years. Lois Broder Greenfield, a psychologist by training who worked with Benjamin Bloom in the late 1940s, was the first person I know about to suggest that teaching the thinking process is as important in engineering education as teaching the content. Among her other contributions, she adapted the thinking aloud process of Claparède with good results. Her chapter provides a historical survey of attempts to teach problem solving. She observes that students' problem-solving skills seem to improve regardless of how these skills are taught. What is important is that overt attempts are made to teach such skills.

Moshe Rubinstein has been teaching problem solving at UCLA since 1969. To the best of my knowledge, he was the first person to offer a formal, interdisciplinary, university-level course in this subject, and 1,200 students now take that course every year. He also has taught "Patterns of Problem Solving" as an American Association for the Advancement of Science–National Science Foundation (AAAS–NSF) Chautauqua course for a number of years, and he has given workshops on the topic all over the country and abroad. Chapter Two, which Rubinstein coauthored with Iris Firstenberg, deals with the tools for thinking that one needs to develop in order to be able to translate what one knows (the knowledge base) into successful problem solutions.

1

Mary McCaulley, a clinical psychologist, was a colleague of Isabel Briggs Myers for years. The Myers-Briggs Type Indicator (MBTI) is a paper-and-pencil instrument that subjects complete to report their psychological type. This instrument, which is based on the theories of C. G. Jung, gives information on how people obtain information and on how they make decisions. These qualities are crucial in problem solving. An individual will fall into one of sixteen MBTI types, and a person's type is generally quite stable over time. McCaulley discusses Jung's theory, provides information on the types of students in different college majors, and gives applications of and strategies for the teaching of problem solving based on Jung's theory.

Don Woods has been a tireless and very effective student of how to teach problem solving. He and his colleagues at McMaster University followed four successive classes of chemical engineering students through their entire undergraduate program a decade ago, and Woods is developing a lower-division course in problem solving based on what he and his colleagues found to be effective. In addition, he edits the *PS Newsletter* and regularly contributes a column called "PS Corner" to the *Journal of College Science Teaching*. He has also presented workshops on problem solving to national and international audiences. In Chapter Four, he discusses what is known about the teaching of problem solving and gives concrete suggestions about how one might go about it.

Jack Lochhead and Art Whimbey have collaborated for a number of years in research on the skills related to problem solving and in applications of this knowledge to the teaching of these skills to others. They have written several books that direct the learner in developing these skills, and they provide a large number of clever, original problems of gradually increasing difficulty upon which to practice. In Chapter Five, they discuss thinking and present the essence of their thinking aloud pair problem solving (TAPPS) technique. The technique has been referred to by others as the *Whimbey pairs technique*; it is an adaptation of Claparède's method. The authors then give several problems, which they illustrate with comments by students trying to solve them, and conclude with a discussion of the costs of teaching problem solving.

Each of the contributors to this volume believes that problem-solving skills can be taught, and in fact all have taught such skills successfully. Each contributor also believes that the process should be taught on purpose. Giving a lot of homework and hoping that students will somehow learn the skills on their own does not work. In these pages is much wisdom, the result of a great deal of observation, reflection, and experimentation by many people over a good many years. You will also find a number of concrete suggestions in these chapters that you can begin to apply in your own classes tomorrow. The authors fervently hope that you will try at least some of their suggestions. You probably will feel a bit apprehensive at first, as everyone does who tries something new in public. However, if you persevere you probably will grow to enjoy the change in the dynamics of the classroom, and so will your students. And, the results may come closer than our current efforts do to what we all thought higher education was supposed to be about.

James E. Stice
Editor

Reference

Young, R. E. (ed.). *Fostering Critical Thinking*. New Directions for Teaching and Learning, no. 3. San Francisco: Jossey-Bass, 1980.

James E. Stice is T. Brockett Hudson Professor of Chemical Engineering and director of the Center for Teaching Effectiveness at the University of Texas at Austin.

Methods used by educators, psychologists, and others to define, describe, or analyze problems and problem solving determine the method used to teach problem-solving skills and determine curricular applications.

Teaching Thinking Through Problem Solving

Lois Broder Greenfield

Educators at every level, educators of every philosophical persuasion, and educators from diverse backgrounds all agree that it is important to teach their students to think, although they may differ about the way in which this goal is to be accomplished. For many, the teaching of thinking is equivalent to the teaching of problem solving, but conflicts arise as to the best way of doing it. The difficulty stems in part from differential concepts and different meanings attached to the term *problem solving* as well as from consideration of the differences among individual problem solvers and among individual problems.

The thesis of this chapter is that the methods used by educators, psychologists, philosophers, and others to define, describe, or analyze problems and problem solving determine the method used to teach problem-solving skills and to determine curricular plans and applications. For the purposes of this discussion, I will adopt the definition offered by Brownell (1942, p. 416): "problem solving refers (a) only to perceptual and conceptual tasks (b) the nature of which the subject, by reason of original nature, of previous learning, or of organization of the task, is able to understand but (c) for which at the time he knows no direct means of satisfaction. (d) The subject experiences perplexity in the problem situation, but he does not experience utter confusion. From this he is saved by the condition

J. E. Stice (ed.). *Developing Critical Thinking and Problem-Solving Abilities.*
New Directions for Teaching and Learning, no. 30. San Francisco: Jossey-Bass, Summer 1987.

described above under (b). Then, problem solving becomes the process by which the subject extricates himself from his problem."

Many methods of analysis have been used to study problem-solving behavior. These methods include analysis of problem solving in animals and in young children, analysis of psychological types or cognitive styles, computer simulation and information processing, rational analysis, and analysis of the problem-solving process. Each of these methods will be discussed briefly, and some applications to the teaching of thinking will be described.

Analysis of Problem Solving in Animals and Young Children

When the premises of behaviorism guided the study of problem solving, animal behavior and the behavior of young children received careful scrutiny. The advantages of studying problem solving in these subjects include ease of observation, ability to control conditions under which the problem solving occurs, and ability to obtain fairly complete information about the background or life history of the subject.

From an analysis of the problem-solving behavior of animals and young children, educators have observed and described much about concept formation, patterns of discrimination, and puzzle type problems. They have also learned about the influence on problem solving of such factors as reward, punishment, motivation, and delay. But, the generalizability or even the applicability of these findings to human adult problem solving is limited in part by the type of problem studied—that is, detours, obstacles, use of tools, mazes, or puzzle boxes—and by differences in mental processes where language is a factor. Although some chimpanzees and young children have been observed to solve problems in similar fashion and although the spontaneous verbalizations of young children seem to give some clues to their process of problem solving, the pertinence of such studies is limited. Woodworth (1938) provides an excellent summary of the work of psychologists who have studied the problem-solving behavior of young children and animals. The observation of both overt and covert trial-and-error behavior, which led to controversy over the phenomenon of insight, has been well documented. Kohler's classic studies with apes, defined by proponents of gestalt psychology as perceptual restructuring, were explained by behaviorists as trial and error. Gilhooly (1982) describes the neobehaviorists, who found simple stimulus-response explanations of behavior inadequate and introduced mediating variables or habit family hierarchies into their descriptions of problem solving. For example, Tolman (1949) added means-end relationships and cognitive maps to this simple stimulus-response explanation of problem solving.

Piaget is frequently cited as the foremost authority on the thinking done by children as a result of his observations and interviews with children. Gardner (1983) provides a summary of Piaget's theories. Piaget takes the position that the baby experiences the world through his own activities and perceptions as sensory-motor operations. At around seven years, the child can perform concrete operations, reasoning about number, time, and space. By early adolescence, the child has progressed to the stage of formal operations, at which he can think logically and develop, test, and revise hypotheses.

Although Piaget's theories have interested educators, particularly mathematics and science teachers, and although they have been used to develop programs to teach thinking and problem solving in the classroom, the theories are weak in some respects. Piaget's explorations are based on problems peculiar to Western culture, and they deal largely with verbal tasks. They assume that the individual stages through which children progress are discrete rather than continuous and that they are all-or-nothing rather than piecemeal. Other investigators have found that the stages of development described by Piaget are not true for all children. In other words, the same child can demonstrate levels of thinking at different stages on different problems on the same day.

Applications of studies of animals and young children to classrooms today are well known and perhaps oversimplified. The work of B. F. Skinner (Stevens, 1951) influenced the development of teaching machines and programmed learning efforts, which were based on the behaviorist laws of effect and of association. Based on exploration of problem-solving behavior in animals and young children, Reed (1939) taught prospective teachers about practice, transfer, incentives, reinforcement, discrimination, motivation, mental habits, and drill. This writer is certain that modern texts still do so.

Analysis of Psychological Types and Cognitive Styles

Various systems have been devised for the classifying of people into groups based on psychological theories, then for relating these classifications to the manner in which people learn, solve problems, and interact with their environment. Disciples of the theorists have developed rating forms, cognitive style maps, and inventories so that teachers and students can determine their own learning styles. Such dimensions as leveling/sharpening, reflection/impulsivity, field independence/field dependence, and scanning/focusing have been used to describe learner strategies or orientations as well as classroom activity preferences.

The implications for the teaching and problem solving of one psychological type indicator, based on the theory of C. G. Jung, have been subject to a good deal of exploration and experimental verification (McCaulley, 1976). McCaulley discusses variations in human behavior based on the ways in which people incorporate information and act on it.

The Myers-Briggs Type Indicator is used to denote the ways in which people become aware (sensing/intuition), the ways in which people come to conclusions (thinking/feeling), the ways in which people take in information and undertake action (judgment/perception), and the ways in which people view the world (extraversion/introversion). Sixteen types can be described, based on the interactions of these four areas. From the perspective of this typology, engineering students appear to differ from other students both in their learning styles and in their methods of problem solving.

Godleski (1984) has used the notion of student type to analyze the responsiveness of students to engineering problem-solving courses. For example, in a chemical engineering course dealing with material balances, intuitive students outperformed sensing students on the unstructured types of problems required in the course.

Currently, researchers are exploring the advantages of using a teaching style syntonic with the learning style of the student. The prediction is that the use of such a style should lead to an increase in both learning and problem-solving ability. However, the lack of clear distinction among categories and a tendency toward oversimplification of the complexities of human behavior pose certain disadvantages.

Cognitive Simulation and Information Processing

There are many similarities between the functions performed by computers and by people solving problems. Both people and computers can store, retrieve, and transform information. They can follow step-by-step procedures to work toward the solution of problems, and they can deal with conditional if-then instructions. In fact, computer simulation of complex mental processes is possible in several fields, such as chess. Computers can be programmed to follow a sequence of steps in the way that the programmer thinks people solve problems (Gilhooly, 1982).

Computer modeling of problem solving directs our attention to the process of problem solving, with problem solving seen as a "process of selective goal-oriented search" (Simon, 1979, p. 365). Computer simulation models have served to elicit psychological theories of problem solving and to ask questions concerning such issues as long- and short-term memory, how knowledge is organized and accessed, and what kind of control system determines the sequence of operations. Computers have been programmed to perform alternative strategies for a single task, and they have been able to model natural language task instructions and rule induction.

In discussing creativity—an important aspect of problem solving—Gilhooly (1982, p. 148) reports that "Simon indicates how the apparent phenomena of incubation and inspiration could be explained in information processing terms by using the notions of familiarization and selective forgetting. . . . He points out the importance of good problem representations—both to ensure search is in an appropriate problem space and to aid in developing heuristic evaluations of possible research directions. . . . Also he reminds us that the rate of progress in science is generally slow, and this fact fits well with the information processing notion of the thinker as a limited-capacity, serial system slowly searching for solutions in a vast space of possibilities."

Applications of computers to the teaching of problem solving have long revolved around the computer as an aid in instruction (computer-aided instruction, CAI), as a learning assistant to diagnose errors, and as a learning coach. Goldstein (1980) describes a model of computer coaching in which the computer uses a model of underlying problem-solving skills to analyze the student's performance. The model encompasses intermediate stages in problem solving as well as typical difficulties that the problem solver might encounter. Computer coaching is more sophisticated than CAI, which presents material based on preprogrammed questions. The coaching system includes the Expert, which results from formal study of requisite knowledge; the Psychologist, which focuses on examining the student's procedures by asking questions and assessing problem complexity; and the Tutor, which senses when a skill has been disregarded by the student, judges whether to intervene in the process, and offers explanations when appropriate. This is but one example of the many explorations currently under way in computer simulation as undertaken by physicists, educators, psychologists, and linguists.

Computer simulation is related to artificial intelligence. Sullivan (1985) reports the interesting observations on artificial intelligence of Arno Penzias, a physicist with AT&T: "The real problem in artificial intelligence systems is the input of data, Penzias said. 'Logic is very good for getting data out. We use logic sorts to retrieve data from our heads.' As an example, he asked, 'What has four wheels all year and flies in the summer?' We get the answer—a garbage truck—from the intersection of two different directions of thought. 'It is very easy to use logic to get this answer out,' Penzias said. 'But it is impossible to use this logic to put it back in. We can take semantic and syntactic information and put it into [the computer], . . . but the dictionary may be saying "you know" a lot more often than you'd think. It assumes a lot of knowledge.' Human brains can store ambiguity, such as a word with a double meaning, Penzias said. 'You must have pragmatic information as well as semantic and syntactic [to grasp the meaning].' In light of this, Penzias questions the use of string-manipulating machines in artificial intelligence."

Rational Analysis

Many analyses of problem solving focus on the answer offered or on the solution given. The advantages of focusing on the product include ease of observation, quantifiability (the answer is either correct or incorrect), objectivity (observers can be trained to a high level of consistency), and reproducibility. The actual method used can be inferred from the product, or it can be deduced by subjective analysis.

The test constructor can also infer process from product, ascertaining by means of statistical techniques the most difficult items, the most frequently chosen incorrect answer, the wording most often missed, and the like. However, certainty with regard to the process employed is not 100 percent. Subjective analysis offers another approach. For example, Dewey (1933, p. 107) has explored the process of thought and analyzed the five phases of reflective thought: "(1) *suggestions* in which the mind leaps forward to a possible solution; (2) an intellectualization of the difficulty or perplexity that has been *felt* (directly experienced) into a *problem* to be solved, a question for which the answer must be sought; (3) the use of one suggestion after another as a leading idea, or *hypothesis*, to initiate and guide observation and other operations in collection of factual material; (4) the mental elaboration of the idea or supposition as an idea or supposition (*reasoning*, in the sense in which reasoning is a part, not the whole, of inference); and (5) *testing* the hypothesis by overt or imaginative action." This discussion presents little evidence to support the case that this is indeed the way in which individuals solve problems. It is doubtful that each individual meticulously observes these five steps in the solution of a problem.

Another rational analysis is offered by Polya (1971), a teacher of mathematics. Polya's analysis is a result of his own efforts to try to understand and explain his and his students' motives and procedures for solving problems. His list of questions (Polya, 1971, front cover) is designed to help both teachers who are trying to develop their students' abilities and students who are trying to develop their ability to solve problems on their own:

UNDERSTANDING THE PROBLEM
What is the unknown? What are the data? What is the condition?
DEVISING A PLAN
Do you know a related problem? Look at the unknown! Here is a problem related to yours and solved before. Could you use it?
CARRYING OUT THE PLAN
Carry out your plan of the solutions. *Check each step.*
LOOKING BACK
Can you check the result? Can you check the argument?

In Polya's analysis, guessing correctly and luck play a significant role.

Rubinstein's (1975) analysis of the general precepts of problem solving involves six steps: Get the total picture, withhold your judgment, use models, change representation, ask the right questions, and have a will to doubt. He further suggests six paths that can be used to generate a solution: Work backwards, generalize or specialize, explore directions when they appear plausible, use stable substructures (modules) in the solution process, use analogies and metaphors, and be guided by emotional signs of success. Based on this analysis, Rubinstein has established a widely respected course on problem solving at UCLA.

Woods and others (1975) describe an adaptation of Polya's approach in teaching problem solving to freshmen engineering students. They observed the problems to which the students were exposed, identified major difficulties that students encountered, tried to identify the necessary problem-solving skills, and tried to teach them to the students. The authors identified a set of steps that combined analytical and creative thinking and used them as a basis for developing and teaching a strategy of problem solving in a tutorial program. Their strategy differed from Polya's in that they inserted a Think About It step between Polya's Define and Plan steps. Leibold and others (1976), volunteer students who participated in the work by Woods and others, elaborated on the Define and Think About It steps: define the unknown; define the system; list knowns and concepts, choose symbols; define constraints; and define the criteria. Students reported some difficulty in applying skills learned in the special tutorial class when they were solving homework assignments.

The strategy is devised rationally. The procedure for improving student skills requires that the students focus on a particular step and then discuss each other's ideas. This method, although it was developed on the basis of a rational analysis of problem solving, emphasizes the actual process. One interesting observation made by the professors who sat in on the required courses with the students was that the lecturers presented a large number of hints for solving problems as well as numerous sample solutions, yet the students did not capitalize on the hints, presumably because they were presented verbally and not written on the board.

Stonewater (1977) points out that, although engineering instructors are well able to specify the problem-solving processes that they themselves use, they may have difficulty specifying the processes that a student should use, since through experience and practice the instructors have internalized so much of what they do. Moreover, the step-by-step procedures that instructors present to students as problem solutions on the blackboard may not be ordered in the way in which the instructor first solved the problem, they may be edited to be more elegant, and the strategy used for problem solution may not be identified.

Stonewater developed an eight-module course called "Introduction to Reasoning and Problem Solving," using a task analysis procedure to develop strategies for problem solving. Three modules were devoted to the preparation phase: discriminating relevant information from irrelevant information, specifying solution, and visualizing the problem; drawing diagrams; and organizing data tables. Five modules presented possible strategies for problem solving: identify unknowns and sequence the solution; develop an organized method for solution; state an assumption which is the logical negation of what is to be proved and use this to contradict given information; infer additional information from what is given; and work backwards. Stonewater reports three concerns in the teaching of problem solving: finding techniques to help students improve their organizational ability, students' abstract reasoning skills, and transfer of learning to other courses.

Other interesting programs using rational analysis have been developed for students from elementary school through college for content varying from mathematics to language arts. Robert McKim (1980) has developed a manual for the teaching of problem solving that emphasizes "visual thinking." He promotes creativity in problem solving, particularly for people in professions with a high visual component, by outlining such strategies as define, persist, cycle, manipulate, and transform. McKim's approach attempts to free problem solvers from overreliance on words and numbers. It forms the basis for college-level courses, but it could be adapted to younger students.

Polya's (1971) directions have been adapted or used by people in fields other than mathematics as an experience-based heuristic designed to understand mental operations that is particularly useful for and relevant to problems of the "problems-to-find" variety. Workbooks, posters, and guides based on Polya's book (1971) are even included in catalogues of educational materials for kindergarten through grade 12.

The "Think About" video series (1979) for the teaching of essential learning skills to fifth and sixth graders presents general language arts, math, and study skills, such as classifying, estimating, and organizing, in sequence and supplements them with special tips aimed at fostering individual problem-solving skills. Programs present and discuss such topics as collecting, classifying, reshaping, and judging information. Teachers are provided with specific hints for helping their students to improve their thinking and problem-solving skills.

Steven P. Meiring (1980) developed a resource for the Ohio Department of Education that was designed to help teachers improve both their own problem-solving skills and those of their students. Meiring's booklets present strategies for helping students begin to solve problems, such as looking for patterns, identifying subgoals, and working backwards, and for solving problems successfully. The overview on the teaching of problem solving, the summaries of related research, and the teaching hints offered in the booklets provide a valuable resource.

The recent trend toward the teaching of writing in all academic areas, often referred to as *writing across the curriculum*, has implications for the use of writing to teach problem solving in technical as well as in nontechnical disciplines. Flower (1981), considering writing as a problem to be solved, contrasted the process differences between skilled and unskilled writers. She suggests that people use the same processes in writing as they do in solving other problems, such as using past knowledge, drawing on strategies that were successful in the past, and exploring alternative methods. Flower stresses the importance in the early stages of writing of defining the problem and deciding on the goal. The six steps for analyzing a writing problem that she outlines have broad application: (1) Define the conflict or key issue. (2) Place the problem in a larger context. (3) Make your problem definition more operational. (4) Explore the parts of the problem. (5) Generate alternative solutions. (6) Come to a well-supported conclusion.

Wickelgren (1974) was heavily influenced by Polya and by Simon. Wickelgren's book, *How to Solve Problems*, has come to be regarded as a classic handbook for approaching college-level math or science problems. He suggests such methods as classifying action sequences, developing subgoals, working backward, and drawing inferences. He drew extensively on then-current research on artificial intelligence and computer simulation.

Analysis of the Problem-Solving Process

Although the explorations and applications discussed in the preceding sections have led to positive results in the teaching of thinking through problem solving, a more productive method of analysis of problem solving focuses not on the conditions or the products of problem solution but on the process as it occurs. This method asks subjects to think aloud as they solve problems. The resulting accounts differ from retrospective descriptions offered after the problem has been solved, which tend to be cleaned-up, edited so as to sound less "funny." The thinking aloud process was first explored by Claparède (Woodworth, 1938), who asked subjects to think aloud as they solved a variety of problems. Claparède showed that problem solving took place in a zigzag fashion, not strictly as trial and error.

Wertheimer (1945) made a contribution to the study of problem-solving processes when he described the development of Einstein's theory of relativity. This description followed the development of the theory, so it is not strictly speaking a study of the ongoing process, but it was based on detailed notes made during theory development. Wertheimer (p. 148n) quotes Einstein as saying, "These thoughts did not come in any verbal formulation. I very rarely think in words at all. A thought comes, and I may try to express it in words afterward." Wertheimer's observations are valuable in describing the process that actually occurs in successful problem solving.

Most subjects given some practice in the method of thinking aloud are able to do this readily. Analysis of protocols obtained in this way reveals individual differences in the method of attack that different subjects use, a variety of reasons for success or failure in reaching a solution, and changes in problem-solving behavior resulting from training or experience. Protocols may differ in completeness or explicitness.

The method of thinking aloud was used by Bloom and Broder (1950) to study the problem-solving processes of college students. These authors asked students from two groups defined as successful and unsuccessful to think aloud as they solved problems. The successful students were those who had high aptitude test scores and who had achieved A and B grades on comprehensive examinations during their first year in college. The unsuccessful students were those at the lower end of both achievement test and aptitude test performance. Based on protocols obtained from the two groups of students as they solved objective types of questions taken from college comprehensive examinations, differences occurred in four areas: understanding the requirements of the problem, understanding the ideas contained in the problem, general approach to the solution of problems, and personal factors in the solution of problems.

Understanding the requirements of the problem pertained to understanding just what problem was posed, that is, to what was required. It involved comprehension of the directions or of the problem statement. The successful and unsuccessful students differed in their ability both to understand what they were supposed to do and to keep this in mind as they worked toward a solution. The successful students were more able than the unsuccessful students to clarify what was involved in the problem, and they had an easier time beginning to attack a problem. The unsuccessful students did not always read the directions. If they read the directions, they did not always understand how to start the problem or what was expected of them. As a result, the unsuccessful students read and reread the directions more often than the successful students did, seemingly in an effort to increase their comprehension. The problem that the unsuccessful students attacked was often not the problem intended by the test writer, either because they misinterpreted a term in the directions or because they failed to keep the directions in mind as they worked toward a solution.

Understanding the ideas contained in the problem concerned knowledge and understanding of the basic information needed to achieve a solution as well as the ability to apply this information to the solution. Although the successful students did in general have more information, the major difference between the two groups was that the successful students were better able to use the knowledge that they possessed to attack a problem. For them, this knowledge could be manipulated, translated, and related to the questions being asked. In contrast, the information that the unsuccessful students possessed seemed to stay in huge, unwieldy blocks that students could apply only in the form in which the information had been learned. The unsuccessful students had difficulty relating their lecture notes, homework problems, and reading to the questions if the questions were asked in a form that differed from their original learning. These students seemed to be unable to conceptualize the ramifications of their knowledge and to assess applications where they were required to change the form from their original learning.

The general approach to the solution of problems related to the procedures that students used as they tried to solve the problems. The successful students differed from the unsuccessful students in three ways: the extent of thought about the problem, their care and system in thinking, and their ability to follow through on a process of reasoning. In regard to the extent of thought about the problem, the successful problem solvers worked more actively on the problems, while the unsuccessful students were more passive in their approach. For example, the successful problem solvers might set up a hypothesis concerning the correct answer or define criteria that the correct answer must meet. Where they encountered an unfamiliar word or phrase, the successful problem solvers might make an assumption about the meaning of the term and use this assumption to work toward a solution. In contrast, the unsuccessful problem solvers made little effort to try to reach a solution. They seemed to find an answer on the basis of superficial considerations, feelings, or impressions. They might try to remember the answer that they had given to a similar problem or just guess at an answer using some vague impression.

The successful students were careful and systematic as they tried to solve problems. They simplified the problems, broke them into smaller parts, and dealt with each part separately. Unsuccessful students were less likely to do these things. They would begin a problem in haphazard fashion, jumping in with no plan and moving from one part to another without apparent plan or direction. They considered the problem as a whole, reading and rereading it, unable to focus on any particular starting point and seemingly unable to develop a plan of attack.

Whereas both groups of problem solvers might sometimes develop a plan for solution, they differed in their ability to follow through on a process of reasoning. The unsuccessful problem solvers might start the problem with a plan, then lose sight of it as they worked toward an answer, seemingly distracted by some difficulty or irrelevancy. In similar circumstances, the successful students might modify their original plan but then use the new plan in their search for a solution.

Attitude toward the solution of problems involved the students' emotions, values, and prejudices as these factors influenced and affected the students' problem-solving methods. Successful and unsuccessful students differed on this dimension in three respects: in attitude toward reasoning, confidence in their ability to solve problems, and introduction of personal considerations into problem solving. In regard to attitude toward reasoning, the successful students valued reasoning as a means for solving problems, whereas the unsuccessful students were more likely to express the view that reasoning was of little value; that is, one either knew the answer, or one did not, and if one did not, nothing could be done. The successful students would work with the problem, revising it or changing it part by part, trying to use the information or skills that they had to make the problem amenable to solution. The unsuccessful students, in contrast, might be discouraged by the statement of the problem or the format. If the statement or the format differed from the statement or format in which their original learning had occurred, they seemed to feel that they could do nothing.

The unsuccessful students had little confidence in their ability to solve problems. If the problem appeared to be complex, they might give up before trying to solve the problem, or they would guess at an answer, hoping that a miracle would occur. The unsuccessful students were easily discouraged and lacked confidence in their ability to solve problems. The successful problem solvers portrayed a positive self-image. By trying more problems, by pursuing whatever leads they could, they were more likely to succeed.

Unsuccessful students were more likely to introduce personal considerations than successful students were. The unsuccessful students would let their feelings or opinions about the problem content, course, or test situation distract them from the problem-solving task. Their personal values colored their answers, even where these values were irrelevant. The successful students were more objective, and although they might voice their feelings or opinions, they were able to separate them from the requirements of the given task.

Whimbey and Lochhead (1982) have based a workbook to teach problem-solving skills on a differential analysis of the skills used by good and poor problem solvers as they think aloud. Models of "good" problem solving are provided on sample exercises. Other exercises ask students to work together in pairs, with one person solving the problem while the other person listens and questions the first student's procedures. The analysis is based on Bloom and Broder (1950). The procedure seems successful; it has been used in engineering classes by Woods and others (1975) and by Stice (1985) among others.

In addition to providing help to students in learning about processes to be used in problem solving, teachers may find it valuable to listen to these processes as they occur. Asking students to think aloud as they solve problems helps the teacher to spot lack of understanding or misundertandings, and it can help to clarify the reasons for students' errors. Teachers can consider the effects of age and experience on the process of problem solving and take the appropriateness of assigned tasks into account.

Listening to students think aloud as they solve problems also helps teachers as test constructors. Statistical analyses point to the items that are answered incorrectly, but by observing students thinking aloud as they answer questions, the test constructor can determine whether the difficulty stems from problems inherent in the test, such as confusing or unclear directions or an unclear statement of the problem, or from students' misreading or failing to read directions, lack of information, or inability to use or transform available information. Listening to students think aloud can help the test item writer to identify items that are incomprehensible to the test taker, although they may be perfectly clear to the item writer. This kind of qualitative analysis can help teachers to perfect their skills as test constructors and help them to develop tests that test the concepts that they have been teaching, not a student's skill in deciphering what the question means.

Use of the Whimbey pairs technique (Whimbey and Lochhead, 1982), whether as a one-to-one remedial scheme or as modified for use in the classroom (Woods and others, 1975; Stice, 1985), seems to be helpful as a method for exploring problem-solving strategies and for alerting students to the various strategies that they might use. The Whimbey pairs technique asks the problem solver to say aloud what he or she is thinking as she or he solves the problem. (The solver does not describe what he or she is thinking about; rather she or he thinks aloud.) The listener observer, whether an individual or a group, listens and asks questions to clarify the process used by the problem solver. The listener observer acts as a sort of mirror to reflect the process and to provide a kind of reality check for the solver. The observer does not act as tutor or teacher. What seems to happen is that the problem solver, by verbalizing his or her thoughts, is forced to provide some structure for these thoughts so that the observer can make sense of them as the problem solver proceeds. In verbalizing his or her thoughts, the problem solver seems to recognize the sense or lack of sense in what he or she is doing and often moves to correct his or her thinking. The technique allows both the problem solver and the observer to focus on the means to the end, the process of solution, rather than strictly on the end, the correct answer.

Others have used the techniques of thinking aloud to develop programs that teach problem solving. Researchers at the University of Massachusetts Heuristics Laboratory have been investigating a variety of instructional techniques for the development of students' cognitive skills and for the teaching of analytical reasoning (Clement, 1976, 1977; Lochhead, 1976). Asking students to think aloud, both Lochhead and Clement study individual students' cognitive processes to determine the learning strategies that they employ, the basic concepts from which they operate, and the techniques that they use in problem solving. They then use this information to help make the students better problem solvers. Lochhead (1976) reports: "We find that what students usually learn from a physics course is not at all what we believed. For example, . . . a student . . . asked me what I did, and I told him I taught problem solving . . . He had taken a physics course the previous year . . . it had been OK but of no lasting value. He had tried to understand the material, but that took too much time and wasn't any use as far as the grade was concerned. So, after a couple of weeks he settled in on memorizing formulas and found that the homework and exam problems could always be solved by plugging the given variables into whatever equation happened to involve those variables. He got some practice in algebra and also in trigonometry, but the physics he learned was just rote formulas . . . There is a popular myth that students cannot understand physics because they are weak in mathematics . . . the inverse is often the case, namely, an ability to do mathematics makes understanding the physics unnecessary. But, students are not the only people skilled at the use of algebra to avoid thinking. We all use the algebra to avoid thinking. We all do it most of the time . . . with rare exception, textbooks and teachers emphasize the mathematical manipulations and spend little effort on explaining the physical concepts or on explaining why the mathematics is an appropriate representation of those concepts." Clement (1977) comments: "One area of physics where these intuitions are particularly strong is Newton's first law. The first law states that a body in motion will remain in motion unless acted on by a force. It is a strange law, because it directly contradicts our own perception. Our everyday experience shows that bodies in motion come to rest without the application of a *visible* force. Furthermore, to keep a body in motion requires the application of a force. Thus . . . Newton's first law implies the unlearning of certain intuitive concepts."

Larkin (1977), Reif (1977), and others associated with the Department of Physics and Group in Science and Mathematics Education at the University of California have contrasted the method of solution used by experts (professors of physics) as they solved physics problems thinking aloud with the method of solution used by novices (students who had completed one quarter of physics). The novice shows a direct approach, that of simply applying various physical principles to the problem in order to produce equations. The equations are then combined to produce the desired quantitative solution. In contrast, the experts do not jump directly into a quantitative solution but rather seem first to redescribe the problem in qualitative terms. The qualitative description is checked against the original problem statement before the quantitative equations that ultimately complete the solution are presented. Novice and expert seem also to differ in the way in which they store physical principles in memory. The novice seems to store such principles individually, while the expert groups together principles that are connected and stores them as chunks. Thus, when the expert accesses one principle from memory, associated principles become available.

Larkin (1977) applied this research to a calculus-based physics course. Larkin stresses that "if one is serious about trying to enable students to solve problems in physics more effectively, the following procedures seem promising: (1) Observe in detail what experts do in solving problems. (2) Abstract from these observations the processes which seem most helpful. (3) Teach these processes explicitly to students."

In an attempt to use group methods to raise achievement to a level comparable with that reached through individual tutoring, Bloom (1984) and his students combined tutoring with mastery learning. The tutoring focused students' attention on higher mental processes, such as applications of principles. Formative tests and feedback emphasized corrective processes rather than mere content or subject matter. The improvement in student performance was marked.

What is the relevance of these reports to the teaching of problem-solving skills? The evidence suggests that educators can help students to learn appropriate problem-solving processes in seven ways:

First, teachers can help students to recognize that problem solving does not progress in a simple straightforward fashion from problem to solution. Teachers might model their own problem solving by thinking aloud on previously unsolved problems, demonstrating that they, too, occasionally run into blind alleys, make miscalculations in arithmetic, transpose numbers, or neglect to consider key terms. In solving problems as students watch, teachers can demonstrate (model) skills that students might strive to attain; occasional errors would serve only to make the processes more believable.

Second, teachers can show it is possible to use more than one method to solve a given problem correctly. That is, they can teach students there is more than one "correct" way of solving most problems and acknowledge alternative creative solutions.

Third, teachers can demonstrate how to break a problem down into manageable parts that the students can solve. As part of this, they can show students how to begin the process by identifying and clarifying key terms, drawing a diagram, or translating the statement of the problem into simpler form.

Fourth, teachers can review the intermediate stages that experts use: redescribing the problem in qualitative terms and calling forth pertinent related material.

Fifth, teachers can break the students into pairs or small groups for practice, with one student solving the problem, and the other student listening, asking for clarification, checking accuracy, and so on, as in Whimbey and Lochhead (1982).

Sixth, teachers can suggest that students develop a plan for solution, including some guess as to the magnitude of the desired answer, before they plug numbers into equations chosen simply because they include the correct variables.

Last, teachers can help students to define or isolate the factors that lead them toward erroneous solutions and develop strategies that can check or counteract these tendencies.

Conclusions

Some interesting and fairly dramatic efforts have been made both to teach problem-solving skills directly and to teach effective remedial problem-solving skills. These efforts differ as a result of the students' experiential background, the teacher's educational theory, or the method of analysis used to determine the components of problem-solving skills. Nevertheless, each effort, no matter what method has been employed for the teaching or remediating of problem-solving skills, succeeds. No matter how problem-solving skills are taught, no matter what educational level at which they are taught, the problem-solving skills of the students to whom these skills are taught improve.

How can this be? Dedicated proponents of each method or theory claim to have the key to exploring and to teaching students to solve problems. And, their methods work! Students do improve their problem-solving skills. A rather simpleminded explanation of this phenomenon is that these diverse approaches lead to improvements in problem-solving skills simply because each pays attention to the process of problem solving. Any kind of attention to such skills and any type of instruction in thinking skills lead to benefits. Ignoring problem solving entirely or assuming that students acquire thinking skills simply by practice in solving problems, drill, or osmosis does not. Thus, proponents of each method for the teaching of thinking through problem solving can claim success for their methods. Let us remember what one outstanding teacher has said: Children and plants grow better if you watch them.

References

Bloom, B. S. "The Search for Methods of Group Instruction as Effective as One-to-One Tutoring." *Educational Leadership*, 1984, *41*, 4–17.

Bloom, B. S., and Broder, L. J. *Problem-Solving Processes of College Students: An Exploratory Investigation.* Supplementary Educational Monographs No. 73. Chicago: University of Chicago Press, 1950.

Brownell, W. A. "Problem Solving." In N. B. Henry (ed.), *The Psychology of Learning.* 41st Yearbook of the National Society for the Study of Education. Chicago: National Society for the Study of Education, 1942.

Clement, J. "An Open-Ended Laboratory for College Physics Students." Unpublished paper, Physics Department, University of Massachusetts, Amherst, 1976.

Clement, J. "On Hobglobins and Physics." Unpublished paper, Physics Department, University of Massachusetts, Amherst, 1977.

Dewey, J. *How We Think.* New York: Heath, 1933.

Flower, L. *Problem-Solving Strategies for Writing.* New York: Harcourt Brace Jovanovich, 1981.

Gardner, H. *Frames of Mind.* New York: Basic Books, 1983.

Gilhooly, K. J. *Thinking: Directed, Undirected, and Creative.* New York: Academic Press, 1982.

Godleski, F. S. "Learning Style Compatibility of Engineering Students and Faculty." In L. P. Grayson and J. M. Biedenbach (eds.), *Proceedings of the Fourteenth Annual Frontiers in Education Conference.* Washington, D.C.: American Society for Engineering Education, 1984.

Goldstein, I. "Developing a Computational Representation for Problem-Solving Skills." In D. T. Tuma and F. Reif (eds.), *Problem Solving and Education: Issues in Teaching and Research.* Hillsdale, N.J.: Erlbaum, 1980.

Larkin, J. H. "Processing Information for Effective Problem Solving." Unpublished paper, Psychology Department, Carnegie-Mellon University, 1977.

Leibold, B. G., Moreland, J.L.C., Ross, D. C., and Butko, J. A. "Problem Solving: A Freshman Experience." *Engineering Education,* 1976, *67* (2), 172–176.

Lochhead, J. "The Heuristics Laboratory Dialogue Groups." Unpublished paper, Physics Department, University of Massachusetts, Amherst, 1976.

McCaulley, M. H. "Psychological Types in Engineering: Implications for Teaching." *Engineering Education,* 1976, *67* (7), 729–736.

McKim, R. H. *Thinking Visually: A Strategy Manual for Problem Solving.* Belmont, Calif.: Lifetime Learning, 1980.

Meiring, S. P. *Problem Solving: A Basic Mathematics Goal.* Palo Alto, Calif.: Dale Seymour, 1980.

Polya, G. *How to Solve It.* Princeton, N.J.: Princeton University Press, 1971.

Reed, H. B. *Psychology and Teaching of Secondary School Subjects.* New York: Prentice-Hall, 1939.

Reif, F. "Problem-Solving Skills and Human Information Processing: Some Basic Issues and Practical Teaching Suggestions." Paper presented at the 85th Annual American Society for Engineering Education Conference, University of North Dakota, June 1977.

Rubinstein, M. F. *Patterns of Problem Solving.* Englewood Cliffs, N.J.: Prentice-Hall, 1975.

Simon, H. "Information Processing Models of Cognition." In M. R. Rosensweig and L. W. Porter (eds.), *Annual Review of Psychology.* Palo Alto, Calif.: Annual Review, 1979.

Stevens, S. S. (ed.). *Handbook of Experimental Psychology.* New York: Wiley, 1951.

Stice, J. E. "Problem Solving: Why Two Heads Are Better Than One." In L. P. Grayson and J. M. Biedenbach (eds.), *Computer-Aided Engineering.* Proceedings of the 93rd Annual Conference of the American Society for Engineering Education. Washington, D.C.: American Society for Engineering Education, 1985.

Stonewater, J. K. "A System for Teaching Problem Solving." Paper presented at the 85th Annual American Society for Engineering Education Conference, University of North Dakota, June 1977.

Sullivan, V. "Are People Still Better Than Computers?" *The Daily Cardinal,* 1985, *93* (50), p. 4.

"Think About." Bloomington, Ind.: Agency for Instructional Television, 1979.

Tolman, E. C. *Purposive Behavior in Animals and Men.* Berkeley: University of California Press, 1949.

Wertheimer, M. *Productive Thinking.* New York: Harper, 1945.

Whimbey, A., and Lochhead, J. *Problem Solving and Comprehension.* (3rd ed.) Philadelphia: Franklin Institute Press, 1982.

Wickelgren, W. A. *How to Solve Problems.* San Francisco: W. H. Freeman, 1974.

Woods, D. R., Wright, J. D., Hoffman, T. W., Swartman, R. K., and Doig, I. D. "Teaching Problem-Solving Skills." *Engineering Education,* 1975, *66* (3), 238–243.

Woodworth, R. S. *Experimental Psychology.* New York: Holt, 1938.

Lois Broder Greenfield, an educational psychologist, is a professor in the Department of General Engineering at the University of Wisconsin–Madison.

*The goal of problem-solving education should be to develop
tools for thinking that will constitute a shell or framework
of action procedures that can apply our intelligence to an
ever-changing knowledge base.*

Tools for Thinking

Moshe F. Rubinstein, Iris R. Firstenberg

There is a prevailing idea that education provides us with a knowledge
base that enables us to deal with life's problems in our professional work
and in everyday life. The reality that we experience does not support this
idea. Too often in this rapidly changing environment, we find that our
knowledge base does not apply, and we are left to our own devices to
acquire a new knowledge base and apply thinking processes in order to
solve problems for which we have no solutions. Problem solving requires
an integrated use of thinking skills and an appropriate knowledge or data
base. The thinking skills and the data on which they operate can be
likened to cooking skills and the ingredients for a meal. You cannot prepare a meal without the ingredients, and you cannot do much with the
ingredients in the absence of cooking skills. Just as outstanding cooking
skills can produce an outstanding meal from limited ingredients, so can
outstanding thinking skills produce novel solutions from limited information. At the same time, poor thinking skills may fail to produce solutions to problems even though there is abundance of appropriate
information. The same can be said for the quality of a meal prepared by a
poor cook who has a rich assortment of outstanding ingredients. Thinking
constitutes the performance skills that we use in order to apply our intelligence to a knowledge base derived from the totality of our experiences.
    It is generally accepted that problems cannot be solved without a
knowledge base. Medical problems can only be solved with a knowledge

J. E. Stice (ed.). *Developing Critical Thinking and Problem-Solving Abilities.*
New Directions for Teaching and Learning, no. 30. San Francisco: Jossey-Bass, Summer 1987.

base in medicine; legal problems, with a knowledge base in law; engineering problems, with a knowledge base in the specific discipline of engineering; and so on. While the knowledge base for problem solving is domain-specific, the thinking skills can be generalized across boundaries between disciplines. The acquisition and development of such general productive thinking skills provide an education suitable for a world characterized by rapid change. A strong foundation in the use of thinking skills in one domain does not guarantee that we can use the same skills in new domains of knowledge. Thinking skills must therefore be made explicit whenever possible, and we must become aware of the capabilities and limitations presented by the human intelligence that we possess. The thinking skills that we acquire should constitute a shell or frame of action procedures that can be applied to an ever-changing data base. It is interesting to note that a number of software companies have developed and presently market expert system shells that come with an empty data base. The data base is generated from interviews with experts in the particular field of knowledge on which the shell is to operate.

The knowledge base and the thinking skills come at different levels of aggregation. Intuitive knowledge of what constitutes a reasonable answer to a problem lies on a higher level of knowledge than knowledge of a fact, because it is developed through experience in a field. Thinking skills that process information on characterizing what the problem is reside at a higher level than thinking about how to achieve a specific objective once the problem has been stated.

Problem-solving ability depends on thinking skills and a knowledge base. But, problem-solving performance also depends on a state of mind, as does learning. We sometimes forget to solve problems. We fail to solve problems because we are unaware of the problems. We do not solve problems because we fear failure. We do not attempt to solve problems because we believe that we cannot. The states of mind that lead to such situations are linked to our attitudes as human problem solvers.

Our growth and development as human problem solvers derives from enrichments of our knowledge base and repertoire of thinking tools and from the cultivation of attitudes that permit us to integrate knowledge and thinking in a productive way. Imaginative tools for thinking will help us to select the direction or channels in which the information in our data base must flow in order to achieve novel solutions to problems. Productive attitudes will enable us to take risks, to overcome fear of failure, and to overcome setbacks in our efforts to solve problems.

To develop habits useful for the acquisition of tools for thinking and knowledge, we must learn to store information in a way that will increase the probability that it can be retrieved when we need it. We must learn to use our tools for thinking to process even incomplete information, and we must monitor for the possibility of changes in our perception of reality. It is the monitoring for change and the willingness to accept change that enable us to learn something new, whether it be a tool for thinking, a fact, model, or an attitude.

In this chapter, we discuss five issues: the role of thinking and problem solving in the era of computers, productive problem-solving attitudes, heuristics that can guide us in the storage and retrieval of information, heuristics for problem representation, and heuristics for problem solving.

Problem Solving in the Era of Computers

Problem solving in the era of computers requires us to focus on the activities that cannot be programmed, such as imaginative perceptions of context and imaginative thinking. We must acquire wisdom to ask appropriate questions, identify goals that are reasonable in the context of human values, and represent problems from complementary as well as from conflicting points of view. To enhance the potential for imaginative thinking, we must learn to spend more time on problem representation before we plunge into a problem-solving mode. We must develop attitudes and thinking tools that enable us to take risks, tolerate errors, and function effectively in the presence of ambiguity.

The age of computers requires us to focus on the unique human capacity to observe, recognize, discover, and spark ideas in the form of untested hypotheses. Motivation is enhanced when we pursue our own ideas, and productivity is promoted by our desire to test their validity. We can use the computer to apply tools for testing our ideas and to perform analysis, extrapolation, prediction, and verification. The scientific tools of logic that can be incorporated into a computer program complement the human ability to observe, recognize, discover, and generate imaginative ideas.

Using imaginative and rational thinking tools, we can develop the capacity to recognize higher order in the form of new patterns and new common principles that unify diverse phenomena and that simplify complex situations. This is the essence of creative and productive thinking and problem solving. Much human endeavor is a quest to make the complex simple.

To maintain our viability in the face of continuous change in the world around us, we must be receptive to new information, we must store and process it, and we must continue to monitor for change. If we accept only information that fits our models and reject everything else, learning stops. Learning takes place when we are receptive to information that does not fit our models. Complacency thrives on harmony. Learning takes place when the stress of conflict created by information that does not fit our models leads us to change them. Imaginative thinking and the courage to make errors can replace complacency with vigilance so that we can act to anticipate change, rather than react to it unprepared.

Productive Problem-Solving Attitudes

A number of attitudes can enhance our potential for successful problem solving. These attitudes include tolerance for uncertainty and ambiguity; willingness to deal with complexity, confusion, and conflict without breaking down; willingness to accept dissonant information; courage to take reasonable risks; and a fundamental desire to enhance our problem-solving abilities.

Creative people have a positive attitude toward problem solving. They consider a problem to be a challenge, an opportunity for new experiences, an enrichment of the repertoire of tools for thinking, a learning experience. With a positive attitude, a frustrated effort to identify a solution is deemed to be compensated for in great measure by the lessons that can be learned when no solution is found. Creative people view an obstacle in a problem-solving situation as a challenge, an intellectual and emotional adventure. Creative people do not run away from complex situations. They tolerate complexity, uncertainty, conflict, and dissonance. They enjoy new experiences. They are more active than passive, and they have capacity for producing results. They are doers. They seem to be in control. They radiate self-confidence.

To increase the potential for a positive attitude toward thinking and problem solving, we can develop guides consistent with human nature and human information processing capabilities that can enhance discovery and creative invention. These guides are called *heuristics*. Heuristics are plausible, provisional, and reasonable, but they are not complete, and they are not certain to lead to success all the time. Heuristic guides and heuristic reasoning can enhance problem-solving efforts most of the time but not always. Heuristics increase the probability of success in arriving at a solution when a solution exists, but they do not guarantee success. Heuristics can point us in the right direction when we acquire and retrieve knowledge, when we represent problems, and when we search for solutions (Rubinstein, 1986).

Heuristics for the Acquisition and Retrieval of Information

In order to acquire the knowledge base necessary for effective problem solving, we need information processing strategies and an understanding of human memory. A number of general guides can help us to manipulate information in a way that will increase the probability that we can retrieve it when we need it and that will make it more likely that we transfer knowledge acquired in the past to new situations in which it is relevant. Like other aspects of problem solving, effort or good intentions to learn material are not enough (Fisher and Craik, 1977). Acquiring information requires work: It requires attention to the material and application of effective strategies.

Structure. In general, an effective strategy is one that makes us organize the information in some way (Lindsay and Norman, 1977). Isolated pieces of information are hard to remember. Structuring new information in such a way as to assimilate it with knowledge already in memory is a very effective strategy for storing information so that it can later be retrieved. Students often comment that introductory courses in a topic new to them require more study effort than upper-division courses that they later take on the subject. The reason is that students in the introductory courses have no structure in memory to relate to. The study effort required for the introductory courses builds such a framework: Upper-division courses relate new data to this framework. Thus, creating memory structures is a requirement for the development of expertise in a subject.

The student must not only give structure to the target information but also understand the structure of the storage system. For example, it has been estimated that a person can only process about seven chunks of information at any one time (Miller, 1956). However, the amount of information in any one chunk can vary, which makes the system flexible and open to increasing amounts of structured information. By understanding the limits of the system, students can learn to initiate effective learning processes. The student, in effect, mediates between the information to be stored and the storage system. Such mediation is accomplished through learning strategies and the general knowledge already in memory.

Montague (1972) argues that mediating strategies alter information so that it fits the structure into which it is placed. In a complementary argument, Bransford and Franks (1976) contend that incoming information alters the existing cognitive structure. Thus, the knowledge base is modified, shaped, and improved. The emerging picture is one of a dynamic system in which information processing plays no less a role than the information to be learned and the storage structure of memory. Building such memory structures requires active processing.

Active Processing. When we are faced with new material to learn, it helps us to paraphrase the ideas, to assess how various facts relate one to another, to ask questions or add comments. In lectures, students often lapse into a court stenographer mode. They get so wrapped up in taking everything down that little processing capacity is left for working actively with the material. Later, when they study their notes, they still do not actively process the material but instead use a passive approach, rereading the notes, underlining in a variety of colors, or copying them neatly, always using the exact same words as the teacher. Such passive, superficial activities are not effective ways of gaining insight into new material, nor do they make it likely that the information will be integrated into memory.

Active Retrieval. Active retrieval is another guide related to active processing that can be used to widen the knowledge base. In contrast to what happens in a computer, active retrieval changes the nature of the information that has been stored (Landauer and Bjork, 1979). The more demanding the effort to retrieve information, the easier it becomes to retrieve the information the next time it is needed. In fact, retrieval is such a potent learning device that it is often better than another presentation of the material. Searching memory for information has been shown to be beneficial even if the target information is not accessed (Gardiner and others, 1973), although the effect is not as great as it is when the information is successfully retrieved. In any case, the practical implication is that testing oneself on material is better than rereading the information an additional time.

Context Effects. The context in which a problem is framed influences the solutions that we consider. Context also has a profound effect on memory. The context in which knowledge is acquired is stored in memory together with the target material, and it can later serve as a guide to retrieval. An amazing range of contextual clues has been shown to be helpful for the accessing of information in memory. We will focus here on general environmental context, as it is the least intuitive. The term *general environmental context* refers to both external factors and internal factors. Studies have demonstrated recall to be better when testing takes place in the surroundings that were present at learning (Smith and others, 1978). Seemingly insignificant factors, such as the size of the room, the amount of light, the presence of other people, and climate, have all been shown to influence our ability to recall information. The effect of learning environment is not limited to physical surroundings. Eich (1980) showed that a learning recall match of internal pharmacological state produced better performance than a mismatch. The practical implication is that in acquiring knowledge that we want to use in unknown future circumstances, studying in a variety of contexts increases the likelihood of a contextual match with the future recall environment.

The Memory Monitor. The complexity of the memory system can be demonstrated when we consider how people answer questions about what they know. There is more to answering questions than looking up the pertinent facts in the knowledge base, retrieving them, and producing them. Consider the following questions: What was Albert Einstein's telephone number? What is the telephone number of your pharmacy? What is your telephone number?

When we ask questions of memory, we find monitoring procedures that analyze whether the relevant information exists, whether it is likely to have been stored, how much effort will be required to retrieve it, and how likely the chances of success are (Lindsay and Norman, 1977). The system does not waste time looking for things that it does not know. It can also judge the cost of retrieving information that is difficult to find. Thus, you refuse to attempt to recall Einstein's telephone number because you know that you do not know it. With respect to the telephone number of your pharmacy, you may believe that you could retrieve the number but that it would require too much effort to be worth the trouble. Because the system knows what the knowledge base contains and what it does not, the monitor can handle the deluge of incoming information by concentrating on the novel, unique, heretofore unknown aspects of the environment.

The monitor that regulates the information base serves another purpose as well. Not only does it judge whether data are contained within the information base, but it also analyzes information that is in the memory store to decide whether it is relevant and appropriate for the situation dictated by the circumstances of the problem. Suppose someone asks, Where do you live? Here are some possible responses: "In the U.S.A." "In California." "In Los Angeles." "Near the beach." "On Highland Avenue." "In the white house at the end of the block." The monitor, which oversees the operation of memory retrieval, determines which answer is appropriate given the circumstances. If you are in Europe and a tour guide asks you where you live, the first answer would be appropriate. However, if you are driving near your home and you are stopped by a police officer who asks where you live, the first answer would not only be inappropriate, it would be considered insolent. Thus, the operation of the memory monitor is as important as the actual storage and retrieval of information in memory.

Heuristics for Problem Representation

One common unproductive approach to problem solving is to move too quickly into a problem-solving mode. There are, of course, situations where quick action is required, but in most cases it is possible to spend some time structuring the problem, presenting it and re-presenting it, each time allowing the new perspective to reveal new elements. Allowing sufficient time for representation is conceptually similar to inspecting an object as one takes a walk around it. What is seen and what is hidden change as one's position changes. A number of guides can help us to take such a walk around a problem and increase the time that we devote to representation. This will make it more likely that we will not embark on a problem-solving mode too soon.

Getting the Facts. Imagine that while driving a truck on a freeway you approach an overpass. A sign on the road informs you that the clearance is twelve feet. A sign posted in the truck cabin tells you that the bed of your truck is twelve feet and two inches high. There is no way to turn back, and there are no side roads. What are you going to do? Most people suggest deflating the tires. However, anyone who would proceed to do so would be moving too soon into a problem-solving mode. The first thing to do is to stop the truck. It is no simple task to deflate the tires without stopping. The next step is to represent the problem. Identify the initial state, the goal state, the obstacles, but do so by getting the facts. Get out of the truck and inspect the clearance with your eyes. Try to measure the height of the overpass as well as the height of the truck. There may be no problem at all.

Get the facts and pay attention to the distinction between facts, opinions, and judgments whenever possible. It is true that to decide what is fact requires judgment. But, in every case where a statement can be verified by inspecting the facts, do so. We often catch ourselves accepting information as factual when it is an expression of opinion or belief. Sometimes, we make an observation, modify it by judgment, and then treat our judgment or belief as fact.

When you are asked for information, be sure that you give facts, not opinions. Such statements as "I think our sales are ahead of last year" or "I believe we tested the equipment before it was shipped to the customer" suggest that more judgment and opinion may be present than fact. When you do not have the key to a closed door that you wish to open, do not conclude that the door is locked and start searching for the key. The prevailing opinion that a locked door can be opened by the appropriate key is one representation that may apply to the situation. Get the facts: Try the handle. The door may be closed but not locked. If this does not work, take a walk conceptually around the obstacle—the locked door in this case. Imagine that you are inside the room. We once suggested this to a friend who was standing in front of a locked door with no keys. He responded by saying, "If I were inside the room, I would have no problem, but the fact is that I am outside." This was indeed a fact, but there were other facts that he had not explored. We suggested that he knock on the door. The door opened immediately. There was someone inside the room who could open the door.

Changing Representations. Change in representation is very often a creative heuristic problem-solving tool. For example, when an obstacle appears to be insurmountable and it has negative features, try to change the representation by focusing on what its positive features could be. It may be very difficult at first to think of anything positive, primarily because your state of mind has been tuned to the negative. But, by going over the facts and by suppressing judgments and opinions, you may come up with new ideas.

Consider, for example, the following story about an apple grower who was about to pick a crop of apples from the trees when a hailstorm hit the area (Flesch, 1951). The hail left marks on the skin of the apples that turned into brown spots. These marks constituted a serious obstacle in attempts to market the crop successfully. It appeared that the obstacle had only negative features. Changing the representation to focus on the possible positive aspects by addressing the facts led to the following line of reasoning: Why did the apples get the brown marks? Because it had hailed. Why then grow apples where it may hail before the crop is harvested? Because apples grow best in mountain areas where chills from storms give the apples a chance to develop the sugars for outstanding taste. In such areas, you may have a hailstorm before the fruit is picked from the trees. The positive feature that was identified from these facts is that the brown marks on the skin of the apples constitute evidence that the apples have been grown in an area suitable for enhancing their sweetness. Therefore, when the grower shipped the apples to his customers, he made sure that each box contained a card with the following information: "Apples grow best in mountain areas where chills from storms toughen the skin and delay the ripening to permit the sugar to develop and yield the most delicious apples. The apples in this box contain evidence that we grow our apples in such an area. The small brown marks on the skin of some of the apples are the result of a hailstorm just before we picked them from the trees. When you taste these apples, you will know how important these chills are in developing sweetness and flavor."

Asking Questions. Language in all its forms is a powerful tool for problem representation. Asking the right question, uttering or hearing the correct word can direct your processing to the appropriate region in your long-term storage from which information that will guide you to a successful change in representation can be retrieved. A particular word or idea may cause you to restructure old knowledge and produce new representations that lead you to creative solutions.

Hammurabi of Babylon changed the course of history by changing the representation when dealing with the problem of an inadequate water supply. Instead of asking how to get the people to the water, he asked how to get the water to the people. This led to the invention of canals. A similar situation arose during the Second World War in Europe when it was necessary to design hangars so that airplanes could be removed quickly in an emergency. It was difficult to achieve a successful solution with conventional hangar designs. An outstanding creative solution was finally obtained by changing the representation and asking how the hangars could be removed rapidly from the airplanes. A folding, mobile configuration for the hangars offered the design solution.

Form and Content. Two fundamental features characterize models in general: a form and a content. It is possible both to describe different contents by the same form and to fit one content into different forms. The choice of form, by which we mean a method of representing a content, determines the ease with which the content can be manipulated and errors of omission and commission can be detected. Thus, the choice of form establishes the facility to refine and improve the model so that it better serves its purpose. For example, the Hebrews and Greeks used letters to represent numbers. This mode of representation was not productive or useful for manipulation of the content that these forms represented. The same was true for Roman numerals. The invention of the positional number system provided a new form that offered much greater power of manipulation.

A change in representation may create a form that is more compatible with our human information processing capabilities. For example, a diagram or a graph may be more suitable than a verbal or a mathematical expression. The new representation can make it easier for us to identify features that were not apparent before the change or that were not easy to see in earlier presentations. These added features may serve as cues to alternative solutions or suggest changes in the goal state by identifying surrogate or proxy goals when we see no way of achieving the desired goal directly.

Heuristics for change in representation include the addition of elements, the removal of elements, the rearranging or combining of elements, and combinations of these activities. A change in representation may involve moving from verbal to visual or mathematical representation or the reverse. We may replace an abstract representation with a concrete representation or the other way around. We may focus on a small part of a problem in detail by ignoring the rest, or we may view the entire problem as a single global feature by filtering out other features.

Heuristics for Problem Solving

A common unproductive tendency in problem solving is to evaluate and choose among a small number of alternatives before sufficient time has been spent generating additional alternatives. Once an alternative has been chosen, you may resist considering additional alternatives and prejudge new alternatives negatively. Therefore, do not begin evaluation and selection of solutions too early.

Concentrate on What You Can Do. Focus attention on surmountable obstacles that block the way to a solution. Before attempting to solve a problem, make sure that you have identified the obstacles. There may be obstacles that can be overcome and others that cannot. In such situations, try to focus on the obstacles that you can overcome, provided that success in overcoming them will lead to the goal.

Consider Implementation. Focus on both quality and acceptability for success in implementing a solution to a problem. The search for a solution to a problem normally receives much more attention than implementation of the solution. This may lead to failure to solve the problem. In particular, when implementation requires the cooperation of other people, it is very important to devote attention both to the quality of the solution and to its acceptance by the agents of implementation. The leaders of the Sony Corporation would not have made their enterprise a success if they had not done just that. They considered tape recorders to be excellent tools for teaching and learning. To market the product successfully, they started by teaching the public about the power of the tape recorder and thus created a market for it.

Maintain Group Harmony. When you lead a group in problem solving, it is important to pay attention to feelings, both to your own feelings and to the feelings of others. Members of the group may disagree about problem representation, problem solution, or both. Disagreement may lead some people to feel hurt and to experience loss of pride. Such people may mount efforts to restore their pride, and this may get in the way of clear thinking and cause them even to reject common sense. To prevent such situations, you must lead the group to recognize that disagreements in problem representation and problem solution are a result of differences in perceptions. The focus on differences in perceptions can help to channel disagreement toward innovation in the attempt to synthesize a consensus from a rich repertoire of viewpoints.

Be a Good Listener. When you interact with others, be a good listener. Try not to formulate your response while you are listening to others talking. Do not judge the ideas of others by saying such things as "You are wrong," "I disagree with you," or "This is nonsense." These statements may promote ill feelings, and they can become obstacles in joint efforts to solve problems. Listen as if you will be required to take an examination on what the other person is saying. Such listening shows respect, and it makes the speaker feel important. It generates good feelings and good will. If you do not agree with the position that a colleague takes, state your own position. It will be evident to you and to your colleague that the two positions are different if you both are good listeners.

Focus on What You Can Control. Identify actions that you can control in a problem situation, and exercise control whenever it can help you to achieve your goals. Studies have indicated that not only actual control but even an illusory perception of control can enhance human problem-solving performance. Giving up control or perceiving that one has no control erodes our ability to perform well and achieve the goals that we have set. When you perceive no choice, you do not disappoint yourself. You act as if you have no alternatives, and the perception becomes a self-fulfilling prophecy. However, when you stop to ask who is in control and what choices you have, you will often be surprised to discover that you have more control than you thought you did. First, we must develop an awareness of our problem-solving styles, whether they are predominantly intuitive and holistic or logical and sequential, and of our ability to tolerate fuzziness, vagueness, and uncertainty. Such awareness will help us to exercise control when a need arises to shift from one mode of problem solving to another, that is, from holistic to discrete, step-by-step detail and vice versa.

Use a Mixed-Scanning Strategy. Use a mixed-scanning strategy similar to that employed by master chess players. The master chess player does well when he or she combines two modes of behavior alternately, going from vague but encompassing scan of the field to a detailed study of a subset of moves and then to further detailed examination of a single sequence of steps that finally leads to a move. This process is repeated each time the player responds to an opponent's move.

In a weather satellite, two cameras perform the functions of broad holistic scan and specific bit-by-bit sequential examination of a small portion of the sky. One camera takes wide-angle pictures covering large portions of the sky in low precision, while a second camera takes high-precision, high-resolution pictures of small portions of the sky identified by the first camera as candidates for closer examination on the basis of some preestablished criteria. This dual scanning involves first a low-precision but all-encompassing scan to look for signals, such as cloud formations or cloud movements, that the second camera can examine in detail.

The investment of time and energy in each mode of scanning depends on the situation, but in general it is important not to persist too long in either mode. Persisting too long in a broad encompassing scan may lead to the onset of boredom and carelessness, and areas worthy of detailed examination may be overlooked as a result. Persisting too long in examining a single detail may blur the overall objective. The key is a flexible, open-ended approach that in scanning the problem domain oscillates between a tacit, holistic, diffused view on the one hand and an explicit, analytical, focused view on the other.

Summary

As the computer increasingly assumes programmable functions, an increasing share of human thinking and problem solving must shift to nonprogrammable activities. These activities include the finding of appropriate problems, the identification of goals in the context of human values, the use of strategies in the acquisition of information that enhance retrieval, the representation of problems and the construction of models from complementary points of view or frames of reference, and the identification of reasonable goals and answers that will do when the "best" answer cannot be obtained within a reasonable time at the cost of reasonable effort or when it cannot be recognized when attained. These nonprogrammable activities require the attitudes and heuristic guides that we have discussed in this chapter. It is true that problems cannot be solved without a knowledge base. But, it is difficult to envision the specific knowledge that will be required in the future. Therefore, the goal of problem-solving education should be to develop tools for thinking that will constitute a shell or framework of action procedures that can be applied on an ever-changing data base. These tools come in the form of heuristics that can be modified and adapted to new situations when appropriate and that can be transferred from one area of knowledge to another.

These activities of problem solving begin with the highly nonprogrammable tasks and progress toward the programmable. But, even after computers and extensive calculations produce results, there is still a need for interpretation of the results, and interpretation is often a nonprogrammable human activity that requires tacit or intuitive knowledge of what is reasonable and acceptable. The nonprogrammable tasks in this area include the holistic, global activities involving imagination, values, attitudes, emotions, and humor. The programmable tasks include sequential, step-by-step, detailed algorithms. The programmable and the nonprogrammable interact. At the beginning, the effort is virtually all nonprogrammable. At the end, the effort is all programmable. The largest amount of mixed scanning occurs in the middle, when we have a reasonable initial grasp of the problem. At this stage, we move back and forth, testing our ideas in a form of mental or computer simulation algorithm and using the results to infer global conclusions or to generate new ideas that lead to changes in the model that we are constructing. Interaction between the human and the computer can enhance problem solving by combining the fertility of human imagination with the power of computer logic.

References

Bransford, J., and Franks, J. "Toward a Framework for Understanding Learning." In G. Bower (ed.), *The Psychology of Learning and Motivation*. Vol. 10. New York: Academic Press, 1976.

Eich, J. "The Cue-Dependent Nature of State-Dependent Retrieval." *Memory and Cognition*, 1980, *8*, 157–173.

Fisher, R., and Craik, F. "Interaction Between Encoding and Retrieval Operations in Cued Recall." *Journal of Experimental Psychology: Human Learning and Memory*, 1977, *3*, 701–711.

Flesch, R. *The Art of Clear Thinking*. New York: Harper, 1951.

Gardiner, J., Craik, F., and Bleasdale, F. "Retrieval Difficulty and Subsequent Recall." *Memory and Cognition*, 1973, *1*, 213–216.

Landauer, T., and Bjork, R. "Optimum Rehearsal Patterns and Name Learning." In M. Gruneberg, P. Morris, and R. Sykes (eds.), *Practical Aspects of Memory*. New York: Academic Press, 1979.

Lindsay, P., and Norman, D. *Human Information Processing*. New York: Academic Press, 1977.

Miller, G. "The Magic Number Seven, Plus or Minus Two: Some Limits on Our Capacity for Processing Information." *Psychological Review*, 1956, *63*, 81–97.

Montague, W. "Elaborative Strategies in Verbal Learning and Memory." In G. Bower, (ed.), *The Psychology of Learning and Motivation*. Vol. 6. New York: Academic Press, 1972.

Rubinstein, M. F. *Tools for Thinking and Problem Solving*. Englewood Cliffs, N.J.: Prentice-Hall, 1986.

Smith, S., Glenberg, A., and Bjork, R. "Environmental Context and Human Memory." *Memory and Cognition*, 1978, *6*, 342–353.

Moshe F. Rubinstein is professor of engineering and applied science at the University of California, Los Angeles.

Iris R. Firstenberg is a lecturer in the School of Engineering and Applied Science and the Department of Psychology at the University of California, Los Angeles.

*A model describing individual differences in problem-solving
styles has practical applications in the classroom.*

The Myers-Briggs Type Indicator: A Jungian Model for Problem Solving

Mary H. McCaulley

The purpose of this chapter is to introduce Jung's (1971) theory of psychological type and the Myers-Briggs Type Indicator as a model for problem solving. The chapter includes an overview of Jung's theory and the
problem-solving model, information about the types of students in different college majors, predictions from the theory about teaching problem
solving to students in different majors, practical applications of the theory
to the teaching of problem solving, and strategies that develop skills in
perception and judgment and thus indirectly help to promote problem
solving.

Jung's (1971) theory of psychological types provides a model that
enables us to understand why people differ in the ways in which they take
in information (perception) and make decisions (judgment). Problem solving can be seen as an orderly way of taking in information and making
decisions. There are many problem-solving models. Most appear to have
been developed by the more analytic of the Jungian types. They have the
strengths of these types, but some overlook aspects of problem solving
that are less salient to the analytic types. The description of the model in
this chapter will allow readers who are familiar with other models to see
how their models fit with Jung's model.

J. E. Stice (ed.). *Developing Critical Thinking and Problem-Solving Abilities.*
New Directions for Teaching and Learning, no. 30. San Francisco: Jossey-Bass, Summer 1987.

Jung's model came from years of observation of people in everyday life and in clinical settings. The Myers-Briggs Type Indicator (MBTI) is the most carefully designed and best-researched of the questionnaires designed to help people access the model by discovering their own preferences for perception and judgment. The authors of the MBTI, Isabel Briggs Myers and her mother Katharine Cook Briggs, developed it in the 1940s and 1950s after two decades of close observation aimed at determining whether the model could clarify people's behavior and life choices. Myers and Briggs collected and analyzed data on more than 5,000 high school students and more than 5,000 medical students before the MBTI was published in 1962 by Educational Testing Service (ETS) as an instrument for further research. ETS collected large samples of college students, and other investigators also conducted research that included many college samples. Isabel Myers and Mary McCaulley established a typology laboratory on the campus of the University of Florida as a center for research. The first conference on the MBTI at the University in 1975 brought 200 people from the United States, Canada, and the Nippon Recruit Center in Tokyo, where the MBTI had been used extensively in helping people to plan their careers.

In 1975, there was a general agreement that the research justified release of the MBTI for practical applications, and Consulting Psychologists Press became the publisher of the MBTI. Since that time, use of the MBTI has increased rapidly in counseling, education, business and industry, government, and the religious community. Jung's observations are used to help individuals understand their own behavior and become more conscious in the ways they direct their lives, to help families and groups understand and appreciate differences among them, to provide information for career planning of young people and adults throughout their work careers, and to develop leadership and teamwork and improve communications within organizations.

In colleges and universities, student personnel staff use the MBTI to match roommates and to plan activities of interest to all types of students, and academic advisers, learning and study skills centers, counseling centers, and career placement centers use it to help students find their best pathway through the choices that they make at each step of their academic careers. All these applications are based on Jung's observation of recognizable differences in perception and judgment. Jung's observations describe characteristics known to all good teachers. The power of his model is that it creates from these familiar observations new patterns that improve the accuracy of our predictions.

Jung's Theory of Psychological Types

Jung's model describes four basic mental powers and four attitudes in which the four mental powers operate. These powers and attitudes combine to produce the sixteen preference types described by the MBTI.

The Four Mental Powers. According to Jung's theory of psychological types, everyone uses four basic mental processes, which Jung calls *sensing* (S), *intuition* (N), *thinking* (T), and *feeling* (F). The sixteen preference types described by the MBTI differ only in the priorities that they place on the processes and in the attitudes in which they typically use each process. Type theory assumes that any conscious mental activity can be classified under one of the four processes.

The terms *perception* and *judgment* are important in the model. Perception includes the many ways of becoming aware of things, people, events, or ideas. It includes information gathering, the seeking of sensations or of inspirations, and selection of the stimulus to be attended to. Judgment includes all the ways of coming to conclusions about what has been perceived. It includes decision making, evaluation, choice, and selection of the response after perceiving the stimulus.

The Two Kinds of Perception. Jung classified all perceptive activities into two categories: sensing and intuition. The term *sensing perception* refers to perceptions observable by way of the senses. Sensing establishes what exists. Because the senses can bring to awareness only what is occurring in the present moment, persons oriented toward sensing perception tend to focus on immediate experiences and often develop characteristics associated with such awareness: enjoyment of the present moment, realism, acute powers of observation, memory for details, and practicality.

The term *intuitive perception* refers to perception of possibilities, meanings, and relationships. Intuitions may come to the surface of consciousness suddenly, as a hunch, as the sudden perception of pattern in seemingly unrelated events, or as a creative discovery. When sensing attacks a problem, it wants to see the facts of the case, the immediate realities. When intuition attacks a problem, it wants to see new possibilities, different ways of viewing the problem, or implications of the big picture. Because intuition sees beyond the immediate experience, persons oriented toward intuitive perception often develop characteristics that can follow from emphasis on intuition and become imaginative, theoretical, abstract, future-oriented, or creative.

The Two Kinds of Judgment. Jung used the terms *thinking* and *feeling* in specialized ways to refer to the rational processes directed at bringing life events into harmony with the laws of reason.

By *thinking judgment,* Jung means the process that links ideas together by making logical connections. Thinking relies on principles of cause and effect and tends to be impersonal. Persons who are primarily oriented toward thinking often develop characteristics associated with thinking: analytical ability, objectivity, concern with principles of justice and fairness, and an orientation to time that is concerned with connections from the past through the present toward the future. Well-developed thinking is the basis for good critical judgment.

By *feeling judgment,* Jung means the process that comes to decisions by weighing the relative values and merits of issues. Feeling relies on an understanding of personal values and group values. Thus, it is more subjective than thinking. (Thinking types sometimes use the word *prioritizing* to describe feeling.) Because values are subjective and personal, persons who use feeling to make judgments are likely to be attuned to the values of others. In decision making, attention to what matters to others can lead to an understanding of people, to concern for the human as opposed to the technical aspects of a problem. It is associated with a need for affiliation, a capacity for warmth, a desire for harmony, and a time orientation that seeks to preserve the values of the past.

The Roles of the Mental Powers in Problem Solving. The four basic mental powers direct conscious mental activity toward different goals: Sensing (S) seeks the fullest possible experience of what is immediate and real. Intuition (N) seeks the broadest view of what is possible and insightful. Thinking (T) seeks rational order and plan according to impersonal logic. Feeling (F) seeks rational order according to harmony among subjective values.

The problem-solving model assumes that the best decisions are achieved when S, N, T, and F are all considered and given due weight. In group decision making, the leader can structure the discussion so that persons who favor S, N, T, and F in their own personalities have adequate time to present their viewpoints before the decisions are made. In an individual, however, a system is needed to prevent paralysis from the contradictory pressures of the four processes, which all pull in different directions.

The needed system is called the *dynamic relationship of the four processes.* Each person uses all four processes, but for each type one of the four processes assumes a dominant role, and its goals become the guiding goals of the personality. The other processes operate, of course, but they are subordinate to and serve the goals of the dominant function. The theory assumes that development of the subordinate functions is an essential but life-long process. The way in which the dominant and other functions interrelate in each type is described in detail by Myers and McCaulley (1985), Myers and Myers (1980), and Lawrence (1982).

The Four Attitudes. In Jung's work, the term *attitudes* is reserved for extraversion and introversion. Myers added two other preferences for orientation to the outer world: *judgment* and *perception.* For the sake of simplicity, extraversion, introversion, judgment, and perception are all classified here as attitudes. Extraversion and introversion describe complementary attitudes showing where life's energy is most likely to flow. Judgment and perception describe the style of living when a person is in the extraverted attitude.

Extraversion and Introversion. Extraversion and introversion relate to the balance of a person's orientation toward the external world of objects and people or toward the internal world of concepts and ideas.

Extraversion (E) describes the attitude when attention seems to flow out—or to be drawn out—toward the objects and people in the environment. There is a desire to act on the environment, to affirm its importance, to increase its effect. Persons habitually taking the extraverted attitude may develop some or all the characteristics associated with extraversion: awareness and reliance on the environment for stimulation and guidance, an action-oriented, sometimes impulsive way of meeting life, frankness, ease of communication, or sociability.

Introversion (I) describes the attitude when energy is drawn from the environment and consolidated within one's position. The main interests of the introvert are in the inner world of concepts and ideas. Persons habitually taking the introverted attitude may develop some or all the characteristics associated with introversion: interest in the clarity of concepts and ideas, reliance more on enduring concepts than on transitory external events, thoughtful, contemplative detachment, and enjoyment of solitude and privacy.

Jung's concept and Myers's descriptions are much broader than the popular views of extraversion and introversion. In popular language, *extravert* means "sociable," and *introvert* means "shy." Jung's theory assumes that extraverts and introverts are normal variants of human beings, recognized through history and literature, and that each type has made major contributions to society. In theory, when extraverts solve a problem, they place greater weight on the situation and the views of other people. In contrast, introverts place greater weight on the conceptual framework in which the problem is embedded.

Judgment and Perception. In the judging attitude, the use of the judging processes, thinking or feeling, can often be observed in outer behavior (that is, the judging processes T or F are extraverted.) In the perceptive attitude, the perceptive processes, sensing or intuition, can often be seen in outer behavior (that is, the perceptive processes S or N are extraverted.)

Judgment (J) can be seen as an attitude to the outer world when a person is concerned with making decisions, seeking closure, planning operations, or organizing activities. Judging types are often characterized as organized, purposeful, or decisive. Perception (P) can be seen as an attitude to the outer world when a person is concerned with seeing all sides of an issue, with not missing anything, and with staying open to new events and changes. Perceptive types are often characterized as adaptable, curious, or spontaneous.

In any new activity, it is appropriate first to begin in the perceptive attitude so as fully to observe or take in the situation. It is then appropriate to turn to the judging attitude to decide on the appropriate action. In problem solving, perceptive types typically remain longer in the observing attitude. Judging types move more quickly through perception in order to reach conclusions. Judging types may therefore decide prematurely that all the evidence is in and thereby close out options, while perceptive types may procrastinate in making their decisions. Procrastination comes from perception with a deficit of judgment. Prejudice comes from judgment with a deficit of perception. Persons new to the MBTI sometimes assume incorrectly that judging types are judgmental. In type theory, the term *judging* refers to decision making, to the exercise of judgment, and thus it is a valuable and indispensable tool.

The Sixteen MBTI Types. The four preferences, EI, SN, TF, or JP, can be combined in a four-by-four matrix to generate sixteen types denoted by letters, such as ISTJ, a type frequently found in civil engineering, or ENFP, a type frequently found among counselors. When individuals indicate their types by responding to the MBTI, they vote their preferences on questions permitting discrimination between E and I, S and N, T and F, and J and P. The theory assumes that the preferences are inborn. However, the theory does not assume that the MBTI reports on the inborn type, since many life events can cause the initial preferences to be developed or diverted. As an engineering colleague puts it, "Type preferences are hardwired, but softwiring can make a big difference in what you see in the adult." Type development is a life-long process that comes by striving for excellence in the two processes that hold the greatest interest and by becoming at least passable in the other two less interesting but essential processes. For all types, the process that is used to engage with the environment is more visible to other people. For extraverts, the dominant or leading process is used mainly when engaging with the environment. (Technically speaking, the dominant is extraverted.) For introverts, the dominant or leading process is used mainly when working in the inner world of concepts and ideas. (Technically speaking, the dominant is introverted.) Introverts use the second or auxiliary process to engage with the external environment. It follows from theory that others see the dominant or best process of extraverts but only the auxiliary or second-best process of introverts. The details of the developmental process and the fine points of the dynamic interactions are described by McCaulley (1981) and by Myers and McCaulley (1985). It suffices here to say that each of the sixteen types is assumed to use daily all four mental processes—S, N, T, and F—and to be able to take all four attitudes—E, I, J, and P. In each type, the theory postulates a specific interaction of these preferences. If we take the opposite types ISTJ and ENFP as examples, Figure 1 shows the key relationships for each of the sixteen types.

In problem solving, ISTJ will want a clear idea of the problem (I) and attack it by looking for the facts (S) and by relying on a logical, impersonal (T), step-by-step (S) approach in reaching conclusions. In contrast, ENFP will throw out all sorts of possibilities (N), seeking feedback from the environment to clarify the problem (E). Brainstorming (NP) will be enjoyed. The human aspects of the problem (F) are likely to be emphasized

Figure 1. Theoretical Characteristics of the Sixteen MBTI Types as Problem Solvers

	ISTJ	ISFJ	INFJ	INTJ
Dynamic Relationship				
Favorite process	Sensing	Sensing	Intuition	Intuition
Second favorite and most visible	Thinking	Feeling	Feeling	Thinking
Least available	Intuition	Intuition	Sensing	Sensing
Weight given to				
EI	Concepts and ideas	Concepts and ideas	Concepts and ideas	Concepts and ideas
SN	Present reality	Present reality	Future possibilities	Future possibilities
SN	Concrete applications	Concrete applications	Abstraction, theory	Abstraction, theory
TF	Impersonal, objects	Personal, human issues	Personal, human issues	Impersonal, objects
Style				
EI	Contemplation	Contemplation	Contemplation	Contemplation
SN	Step-by-step, linear	Step-by-step, linear	Back and forth, global	Back and forth, global
TF	Analyze logically	Weigh values	Weigh values	Analyze logically
JP	Organize, seek closure	Organize, seek closure	Organize, seek closure	Organize, seek closure

	ISTP	ISFP	INFP	INTP
Dynamic Relationship				
Favorite process	Thinking	Feeling	Feeling	Thinking
Second favorite and most visible	Sensing	Sensing	Intuition	Intuition
Least available	Feeling	Thinking	Thinking	Feeling
Weight given to				
EI	Concepts and ideas	Concepts and ideas	Concepts and ideas	Concepts and ideas
SN	Present reality	Present reality	Future possibilities	Future possibilities
SN	Concrete applications	Concrete applications	Abstraction, theory	Abstraction, theory
TF	Impersonal, objects	Personal, human issues	Personal, human issues	Impersonal, objects
Style				
EI	Contemplation	Contemplation	Contemplation	Contemplation
SN	Step-by-step, linear	Step-by-step, linear	Back and forth, global	Back and forth, global
TF	Analyze logically	Weigh values	Weigh values	Analyze logically
JP	Discover, adapt	Discover, adapt	Discover, adapt	Discover, adapt

	ESTP	ESFP	ENFP	ENTP
Dynamic Relationship				
Favorite process and most visible	Sensing	Sensing	Intuition	Intuition
Second favorite	Thinking	Feeling	Feeling	Thinking
Least available	Intuition	Intuition	Sensing	Sensing
Weight given to				
EI	External situation	External situation	External situation	External situation
SN	Present reality	Present reality	Future possibilities	Future possibilities
SN	Concrete applications	Concrete applications	Abstraction, theory	Abstraction, theory
TF	Impersonal, objects	Personal, human issues	Personal, human issues	Impersonal, objects
Style				
EI	Talk and action	Talk and action	Talk and action	Talk and action
SN	Step-by-step, linear	Step-by-step, linear	Back and forth, global	Back and forth, global
TF	Analyze logically	Weigh values	Weigh values	Analyze logically
JP	Discover, adapt	Discover, adapt	Discover, adapt	Discover, adapt

	ESTJ	ESFJ	ENFJ	ENTJ
Dynamic Relationship				
Favorite process and most visible	Thinking	Feeling	Feeling	Feeling
Second favorite	Sensing	Sensing	Intuition	Intuition
Least available	Feeling	Thinking	Thinking	Feeling
Weight given to				
EI	External situation	External situation	External situation	External situation
SN	Present reality	Present reality	Future possibilities	Future possibilities
SN	Concrete applications	Concrete applications	Abstraction, theory	Abstraction, theory
TF	Impersonal, objects	Personal, human issues	Personal, human issues	Impersonal, objects
Style				
EI	Talk and action	Talk and action	Talk and action	Talk and action
SN	Step-by-step, linear	Step-by-step, linear	Back and forth, global	Back and forth, global
TF	Analyze logically	Weigh values	Weigh values	Analyze logically
JP	Organize, seek closure	Organize, seek closure	Organize, seek closure	Organize, seek closure

44

over impersonal, technical issues (T). To the ISTJ, the ENFP approach is likely to seem irrational or scattered. To the ENFP, the ISTJ approach is likely to seem slow and unimaginative.

How the Model Applies to Problem Solving

Figure 1 also shows how the sixteen types are likely to differ in the strategies that they use for solving problems. At first glance, the diversity of sixteen types can seem discouraging to the teacher faced with teaching problem solving in a short time to a large number of students. On closer inspection, the reader will see that there are few variables and that there is an order to their appearance. In this section I adapt the problem-solving model of Myers (1980) for the four mental processes and supplement it with input from the attitudes. The model was first described in *Introduction to Type* (Myers, 1980), a pamphlet that explains type theory to the general public; it is a useful teaching aid when the MBTI is used in the classroom. Myers believed that if young people can learn to follow the model, they will gain greater command and flexibility in using their mental powers and thereby make better decisions and become more effective in all aspects of their lives.

Strategies for Using the Model. Use one process at a time. (Muddled thinking comes from using more than one process at the same time.) Use each process consciously and with purpose. (Don't just spin your wheels.) Use each process in its own area. (Don't use sensing for seeking new possibilities or feeling to analyze an equipment problem.) Don't let other processes interfere. (If you are using sensing to see the realities, temporarily put intuition aside.) Use the processes in the following order: sensing, intuition, thinking, feeling. (There is debate about this injunction. Some types insist they find other orders more useful. However, the internal logic of this order is useful in teaching the model to students.)

Steps in Problem Solving. First, use sensing to face the facts, to be realistic, to find exactly what the situation is, to see your own actions, and to see other people's actions. Do not let wishful thinking or sentiment blind you to the realities. Second, use intuition (N) to discover all the possibilities, to see how you might change the situation, to see how you might handle the situation differently, and to see how other people's attitudes might change. Try not to assume that you have been doing the only obviously right thing. Third, use thinking (T) to make an impersonal analysis of the problem; to look at causes and their effects; to look at all the consequences, both pleasant and unpleasant; to count the full costs of possible solutions; and to examine misgivings you may have been suppressing, because of your loyalties to others or because you don't like to admit you may have been wrong. Fourth, use feeling (F) to weigh how deeply you care about what your choice will gain or lose; to put more weight on permanent than on temporary effects, even if the temporary effects are more attractive right now; to consider how other people will feel, even if you think they are unreasonable; and weigh other people's feelings and your own feelings in deciding which solution will work best.

Myers's comments to users of the exercise help teachers to appreciate why different types of students respond differently to the steps just outlined. After describing the four steps, Myers (1980, p. 4) added: "You will probably choose, as usual, a solution that appeals to your favorite process but on a sounder basis than usual, because you will have considered facts, possibilities, consequences, and human values. Ignoring any of these can lead to trouble. Intuitives may base a decision on some possibility without discovering facts which will make it impossible. Sensing types may settle for a faulty solution to a problem because they assume no better one is possible. Thinking types may ignore human values, and feeling types may ignore consequences. You will find some steps in this exercise easier than others. The ones that use your best processes are rather fun. The others are harder but worthwhile. If feeling is your favorite process, the attempt to see *all* the consequences of an act may show you that even the best intentions can go wrong unless thought through. If thinking is your favorite process, the attempt to learn how others *feel* about your plans may show why you meet so much opposition. What makes the hard steps hard is that they call for the strengths of types opposite to your own. When your problem is important, you may be wise to consult someone to whom these strengths come naturally. It is startling to see how different a given situation can look to a person of opposite type, but it will help you to understand and use the neglected opposite side of yourself."

Using the Attitudes in Problem Solving. First, use extraversion (E) to see events in your environment that may influence the problem, to seek people who may have information about the problem, and to talk out loud about the problem as a way of clarifying your ideas. Second, use introversion (I) to consider ideas that may have a bearing on the problem, to look for eternal truths that may be obscured by current fads, and to take time alone to think deeply about the problem. Third, use judgment (J) to stay on track and not be diverted into side issues, to plan ahead so as not to be caught in a last-minute rush, and to push yourself and others toward a solution. Fourth, use perception (P) to make sure that you have looked at all aspects of the problem, to keep your eyes open to new developments that might affect the decision, and to avoid jumping to conclusions before the facts are in.

This brief overview of the model, like all overviews, ignores many complexities, but it does provide a framework for helping students individually and in groups to improve their problem-solving abilities.

Facts About Types of Students in Colleges and Fields of Study

Teachers planning to use type concepts to teach problem solving will find it useful to estimate the type distribution of students. A problem-solving exercise designed to develop logical thinking may work better in an engineering class, where thinking types are likely to be in the majority, than in an elementary education course, where feeling types are typically in the majority. Almost every classroom will have representatives from all sixteen types, so teachers need flexibility of approach. The following facts are derived from research with the MBTI, including McCaulley and Natter (1974), McCaulley (1976), McCaulley and others (1983), Blaylock (1980; 1983), Nisbet and others (1982), Hoy and Boulton (1983), and Yokomoto and Ware (1982; 1984). Many more facts can be found in Myers and McCaulley (1985).

Extraverts and Introverts. Extraverts outnumber introverts in the general population by a ratio ranging between two to one and three to one. Relatively more introverts continue on to higher education, since higher education is concerned with concepts and ideas. The proportion of introverts increases at each level of education for students and for their faculty. In our sample of 2,282 college teachers, 54 percent preferred introversion. In college majors, extraverts are somewhat more attracted to education, business, and journalism and to fields requiring outside activity, extensive contact with people, or both. Introverts are somewhat more attracted to engineering, the arts, sciences, and humanities.

Sensing and Intuitive Types. In the general population, sensing types outnumber intuitive types by a ratio of approximately three to one. Intuitives are more attracted to higher education, since it tends to require intuitive skills of abstract conceptualization. For both students and faculty, the higher the level of education, the greater the proportion of intuitive types. In the sample of 2,282 college and university teachers, 64 percent preferred intuition. Samples of National Merit finalists, Florida Future Scientists, and Phi Beta Kappas show intuitive types to be in the majority. Intuitive types are more attracted to independent study programs and to fields requiring use of theory, abstraction, imagination, or use of symbols, including the arts, humanities, sciences, behavioral sciences, and other fields requiring communications skills. In contrast, sensing types are attracted to fields that require practical, hands-on skills, such as civil engineering, accounting, orthopedic surgery, pharmacy, patient care, and education, especially in the early grades.

Thinking and Feeling. Male samples typically have more thinking types (usually from 55 to 65 percent), and female samples have more feeling types (usually 65 to 75 percent). Majors attractive to thinking types include engineering, the sciences, technical fields, and business. Majors attractive to feeling types include helping professions, teaching, communications, and the humanities.

Judgment and Perception. In the general population, judging types are slightly in the majority, roughly 55 percent. There are fewer significant differences among judging and perceptive types in college majors than there are for the other preferences. However, judging types are attracted to fields in which system and order are important, such as engineering, business, and the health professions. Perceptive types are more likely to choose fields where adaptability and curiosity are important, such as advertising, psychology, or the fine arts.

Summary. This brief overview is not intended to be comprehensive. It is designed only to permit college teachers to make educated guesses as to the likely composition of their classes. Of the four preferences, sensing-intuition is most important to the teacher, since it is the SN preference that describes what aspect of a situation is salient and interesting. Sensing and intuitive types attack problems from opposite directions: Sensing types move from the specific to the general, while intuitive types move from the grand design to the details. In fields with relatively equal numbers of S and N students, such as engineering, the faculty have more of a challenge maintaining student interest than in fields, such as counseling, where students and faculty are more similar.

Practical Applications of the MBTI Model to the Teaching of Problem Solving

This section gives some examples of strategies that faculty are using to teach problem solving. There are two main goals in using the model with students: to improve students' problem-solving skills and to help students to gain respect for others whose minds work differently from their own. Implicitly or explicitly the teacher is conveying examples of the constructive use of differences. It is unfortunate that in our democratic society the word *different* is often used pejoratively. Our aim is for the response to the statement "You certainly are different!" to become "Yes, many different talents are needed in our diverse society" or "Indeed, and isn't it interesting that we can be at the same event and see it so differently?"

Many colleges and universities have staff in their counseling center or psychology department who are knowledgeable about the MBTI. It is often possible to work out ways for counselors to administer the MBTI and explain it to a class in preparation for use of the theory to design problem-solving activities without asking students to take the MBTI.

Example 1: Group Problem Solving. This exercise assumes that students have information about their types and that they have read about problem solving and constructive use of differences in the booklet *Introduc-*

tion to Type (Myers, 1980). Faculty can use any problem from the course content. For example, how can the United States balance the budget? Why did Hamlet take so long to act? How would you introduce a new process on a production line? How would you present this idea to the citizenry? Business courses often use management games that are specifically designed to teach problem solving.

The teacher assigns students to type-alike groups. The assignment depends to some extent on the type distribution of the class. Sometimes one type is so well represented that a group can consist entirely of members of that type. Sometimes a type is so rare that the group must be made up of kindred types. Ways of grouping the types are described by Myers and McCaulley (1985). The following combinations of perception and judgment—ST types: practical and matter of fact, SF types: sympathetic and friendly, NF types: enthusiastic and insightful, NT types: logical and ingenious—are especially useful in teaching problem solving. They are described in Myers (1980). The teacher assigns the same problem to student groups, using between three and eight sets of directions, depending on the time available for processing the four functions and four attitudes.

Apply Sensing Perception. Next, the teacher asks each group to come up with a statement of the facts that are necessary for reaching a solution. These may be facts that the teacher has supplied, or they may be facts that the students would have seek in order to solve the problem. The teacher has each group report out the group consensus. (Newsprint is useful. As an alternative, each group may prepare a handout for other members of the class.) With the teacher's help, the students review group differences. S groups often list many facts or concrete aspects of the problem. N groups sometimes list a possibility as if it were a fact.

Apply Intuitive Perception. The teacher now asks the groups to come up with as many possibilities or options as possible. They are to brainstorm but not to criticize any suggestion at this stage. Again, the groups report out. The teacher guides observations of how the groups differ. N groups typically report more possibilities and more extreme leaps than S groups do.

Apply Thinking Judgment and Feeling Judgment. The class now takes the ideas generated thus far, and each group seeks the best solutions. They are instructed to use thinking first and then feeling, using the instructions given in the first section of this chapter. If there is time, T and F can be processed separately. As the groups report out, the teacher helps them to identify T and F differences. It is helpful to point to key words that differentiate T logical objectivity from F values. The groups help each other to assess the adequacy of the logic of various T choices and the level of discrimination of the values reflected in F choices. (Beginners often profit by assessing whether an F decision gave priority to short-range or long-range values.)

Apply the Attitudes. Each group probably includes both extraverts and introverts as well as students preferring judgment and students preferring perception. Students reflect on the process that they used to solve the problem. Who focused on the characteristics of the situation and sought a solution by changing objects or events (E)? Who looked for a clear conceptual framework (I)? Group members also try to identify and contrast the processes of staying open and maintaining curiosity about options (P) with the feeling of pressure to come to closure (J). Problems that require action plans to implement the solution are excellent vehicles for identifying and practicing E and I, J and P. As students weigh the effects of different strategies, they come to see where their natural strategy is more successful and where they will benefit from seeking modes other than the ones that come naturally to mind.

Example 2: Learning from Homework Assignments. The model can be used to organize classroom discussions that are not explicitly problem-solving tasks. Students can be grouped as in exercise 1 to discuss homework assignments. Each group is asked to summarize the salient points in the assignment. Natter (1974) describes the typical result: The logical and ingenious NT types list the broad conceptual logical models, the practical and matter-of-fact ST types carefully define new terms and list new facts, the enthusiastic and insightful NF types may draw pictures or write poetry to exemplify the underlying meaning of the assignment, and the sympathetic and friendly SF types can enjoy the interaction of the discussions so much that they find it hard to remain on task.

The feedback of the groups to one another provides striking confirmation of the fact that people can view the same event very differently. This insight provides material for more exciting class discussions and a deeper understanding of the assignment than any group would have achieved alone.

Example 3: Using the Model to Assess Problem Solving in Class Material. The model can be used even when students have not answered the MBTI and even when they have not been formally introduced to type concepts. Courses in business, economics, political science, history, and the physical sciences provide many examples of people solving problems. The teacher can guide the discussion, using the model to analyze the use of S, N, T, and F and the orientation toward E, I, J, and P styles of decision making. Imperfect solutions can be analyzed to see if any process was neglected. For example, Tuchman (1984) describes the difficulties that arise when decision makers fail to look objectively at the facts (S). Courses concerned with literary characters or the media can use the model to analyze the problem solving of fictional characters. In George Eliot's *The Mill on the Floss* (1962), Tom Tulliver, who has all the characteristics of an extravert who prefers sensing, struggles mightily with Latin and Euclid, two subjects that require use of introversion and intuition. His intuitive sister Maggie is enchanted at Tom's studies and hungry to learn what he rebels at being taught. Any topic concerned with human misunderstandings can be enriched if it is approached from the viewpoint of type differences.

Example 4: Task Groups in the Classroom. Lee Harrisberger uses the MBTI in a mechanical engineering design clinic to teach professional skills to senior engineering students (McCaulley and others, 1983). Student teams are assigned real-world problems with client companies. Prior to these assignments, students have learned each others' types; a type distribution has been posted for reference during class discussions. Teams use knowledge of type to evaluate team projects and as a tool to improve their communications with each other and with the client. The teacher assists by drawing their attention to type differences that impede communication or problem solving. The teacher emphasizes that everyone has to be able to use all four processes and all four attitudes. The MBTI describes the style that each student is most likely to use as his or her first approach to a problem. Nevertheless, the preferred style may be a poor one to use in some engineering situations, and the student may need to adopt other styles temporarily in order to get the job done. Because the task forces are dealing with real problems, composition is heterogeneous as to type. Homogeneous teams may find it easy to communicate, but it is likely that they lack the diversity of skills needed for good problem solving (Blaylock, 1983).

Example 5: Examination of the Learning Process Itself. Faculty and students benefit from an examination of the process of learning in the classroom. What made a class interesting or dull? What made it clear or confusing? Feedback in terms of type differences leads to insights for students and to valuable information for the teacher.

Students in research courses may be amused and instructed by Peters's (1981) discovery that the ST, SF, NF, and NT graduate students disagreed in predictable directions on what was "good" research. Each group liked the research that had been judged to characterize its own style. The logical and ingenious NTs tended to prefer research with clearly defined theoretical models. Practical and matter-of-fact STs preferred research of a clearly defined problem with thorough data analysis. Enthusiastic and insightful NF students preferred research that had important implications for human problems. Sympathetic and friendly SF students liked the research of the NFs but preferred a case study approach to research. Each group made remarks that were somewhat critical of the research of opposite styles. For example, the NFs found the ST research dry and meaningless, while the STs thought that the NF ideas might be useful if only someone would design a tight study that could test them properly. Graduate students and faculty find Peters's research helpful in bringing amusement and objectivity to discussions that can provoke acrimonious debate.

Strategies for Teaching the Components of the Model

Teachers who know the model can use many ongoing activities to improve command of S, N, T, and F in the day-to-day activities of the classroom. If the students know their types, the teacher can ask them to find links between the assignment and the model. Even if students do not know their types, the teacher can use the model to guide discussions or to plan the teaching in order to develop students' maturity in the use of a process.

Careful observation, in the physical sciences, and use of materials, in engineering and the fine arts, can be used to develop sensing (S). Generating hypotheses, looking at problems from new angles or for subtle implications, and finding meanings that fit best when translating from another language help to develop intuition (N). Procedures of arithmetic and mathematics, courses in logical thinking, work with the physical properties of tangible objects, indeed any activity in any course where cause-effect relationships are clear, can be used to develop thinking (T). Any activity that weighs the relative benefits of short-range and long-range good, comparisons to develop discriminating taste in the arts, and discussions of the values that entered into the decisions of historical or literary characters help to develop feeling (F). Exercises that require interviewing or action outside the classroom develop extraversion (E). Exercises that require understanding of the concepts underlying events promote introversion (I). Discussion of situation ethics fosters E, while discussion of ethical principles develops I. Finally, exercises that require outlining, organizing, or classifying develop judgment (J), while exercises that require exploration without guidelines or planning promote perception (P).

The discussion here is meant to provide just enough information about the model and its applications to whet the reader's appetite. In my experience, many teachers who grasp the model see their entire curriculum and teaching in a new light. They report that teaching becomes challenging and fun again as they see ways of reaching the widely different minds before them.

Teachers who face a class with a broad range of types are less frustrated when they realize that it is difficult to keep different types at the same level of interest. Teachers who face a class where almost everyone is similar to themselves at first find it invigorating to be so readily understood. Initial complacency is often followed by a conscious effort to help the class avoid the blind spots of a homogeneous group. For example, a science class made up mainly of intuitive, thinking NT types can easily overlook the way their solutions will appear to people concerned with practical, personal SF applications. Teachers face both diversity and homogeneity with groups of engineering students, who tend to have more introverts, thinking types, and judging types, with about equal numbers

52

of sensing and intuitive types. The substantial numbers of S students and N students provide a challenge, since the S students tend to want to begin from the facts and move step by step from those facts toward a solution. In contrast, the intuitives want to start from the big picture and work back. The large numbers of TJ students and faculty in engineering can lead to a useful emphasis on organized work habits and logical, tough-minded approaches to problems. However, the TJ classroom provides little support and considerable stress for the less frequent FP students. The TJ teachers can inadvertently focus so much on the logical, analytical, organized TJ ways of solving problems that their students receive little preparation in the interpersonal skills that they will need on the job—the abilities to listen to people (F), to be alert for new developments (E and P), and to take human values (F) as well as technical issues (T) into account. A more conscious use of type in engineering will not only help the more frequent TJ students to become accomplished problem solvers but will give the less frequent FP students an appreciation of the value of their approach to engineering.

In summary, MBTI users believe that students who learn to use the model in their daily activities will see the world more accurately, develop better alternatives, make fewer decisions that have unintended consequences, and feel more attuned to their own values and to what matters to other people. As a result, throughout their lives they will make better work and personal decisions and be a more positive force in our democratic society.

References

Blaylock, B. K. "Interactive Effects of Classificatory and Environmental Variables in Decision Making Under Conditions of Risk." Unpublished doctoral dissertation, Georgia State University, 1980.

Blaylock, B. K. "Teamwork in a Simulated Production Environment." *Research in Psychological Type*, 1983, *6*, 58–67.

Eliot, G. *The Mill on the Floss.* New York: Collier Books, 1962.

Hoy, F., and Boulton, W. R. "Problem-Solving Styles of Students: Are Educators Producing What Business Needs?" *Collegiate News and Views*, 1983, *36*, 15–21.

Jung, C. G. *Psychological Types.* (H. G. Baynes, Trans., rev. R.F.C. Hull.) Princeton, N.J.: Princeton University Press, 1971.

Lawrence, G. D. *People Types and Tiger Stripes: A Practical Guide to Learning Styles.* (2nd ed.) Gainesville, Fla.: Center for Applications of Psychological Type, 1982.

Lawrence, G. D. "A Synthesis of Learning Style Research Involving the MBTI." *Journal of Psychological Type*, 1984, *8*, 2–15.

McCaulley, M. H. "Psychological Types in Engineering: Implications for Teaching." *Engineering Education*, 1976, *67* (7), 729–736.

McCaulley, M. H. "Jung's Theory of Psychological Type and the Myers-Briggs Type Indicator." In P. McReynolds (ed.), *Advances in Psychological Assessment V.* San Francisco: Jossey-Bass, 1981.

McCaulley, M. H., Godleski, E. S., Yokomoto, C. F., Harrisberger, L., and Sloan, E. D. "Applications of Psychological Type in Engineering Education." *Engineering Education*, 1983, *73*, 394–400.

McCaulley, M. H., and Natter, F. L. "Psychological (Myers-Briggs) Type Differences in Education." In F. L Natter and S. A. Rollin (eds.), *The Governor's Task Force on Disruptive Youth: Phase II*. Tallahassee, Fla.: Office of the Governor, 1974.

Myers, I. B. *Introduction to Type.* (3rd ed.) Palo Alto, Calif.: Consulting Psychologists Press, 1980.

Myers, I. B., and McCaulley, M. H. *Manual: A Guide to the Development and Use of the Myers-Briggs Type Indicator.* Palo Alto, Calif.: Consulting Psychologists Press, 1985.

Myers, I. B., and Myers, P. B. *Gifts Differing.* Palo Alto, Calif.: Consulting Psychologists Press, 1980.

Natter, F. L. Personal communication, 1974.

Nisbet, J. A., Ruble, V. E., and Schurr, K. T. "Predictors of Academic Success with High-Risk College Students." *Journal of College Student Personnel*, 1982, *23*, 227–235.

Peters, C. E. "An Investigation of the Relationship Between Jungian Psychological Type and Preferred Styles of Inquiry." Unpublished doctoral dissertation, Ohio State University, 1981.

Tuchman, B. W. *The March of Folly.* New York: Knopf, 1984.

Yokomoto, C. F., and Ware, J. R. "Improving Problem-Solving Performance Using the MBTI." In L. P. Grayson and J. M. Biedenbach (eds.), *Proceedings of the 90th Annual Conference of the American Society for Engineering Education*, vol. 1. Washington, D.C.: American Society for Engineering Education, 1982.

Yokomoto, C. F., and Ware, J. R. "Individual Differences in Cognitive Tasks." In L. P. Grayson and J. M. Biedenbach (eds.), *Proceedings of the Fourteenth Annual Frontiers in Education Conference*. Washington, D.C.: Institute of Electrical and Electronics Engineers and American Society for Engineering Education, 1984.

Mary H. McCaulley, a clinical psychologist and former member of the faculty of the University of Florida, is president of the Center for Applications of Psychological Type in Gainesville, Florida. She worked closely with the developer of the Myers-Briggs Type Indicator for more than a decade, and she is coauthor of the MBTI Manual.

Options for the teaching of thinking and problem-solving
skills are contrasted, and practical suggestions about ways of
developing our students' problem-solving skills are presented.

How Might I Teach
Problem Solving?

Donald R. Woods

We all solve problems. We all teach problem solving to our students. But do we? This chapter discusses some definitions of problem solving, summarizes some research about the teaching of problem solving, explores some options, and gives some ideas about what we could do in the classroom.

Here is one possible definition of problem solving: Problem solving is the mental process that we use to arrive at a "best" answer to an unknown or some decision, subject to a set of constraints. The problem situation is not one that has been encountered before; we cannot recall from memory a procedure or a solution from past experience. We have to struggle to obtain a "best" answer.

The skills needed in this process include a knowledge base pertinent to the content of the problem; the ability to identify, locate, obtain, and evaluate missing information; the ability to learn on one's own; such thinking skills as analysis (classify, check for consistency, reason, and identify relationships), creativity, ability to generalize and to simplify and broaden perspectives; such attitudes as motivation and perseverance; ability to cope with ambiguity, fear, anxiety, and procrastination; interpersonal and group skills; communication skills; and an awareness of how one thinks, one's personal preference or style when learning or processing information. In addition, we use an organized approach (or a strategy) and a host of heuris-

J. E. Stice (ed.). *Developing Critical Thinking and Problem-Solving Abilities.*
New Directions for Teaching and Learning, no. 30. San Francisco: Jossey-Bass, Summer 1987.

tics or hints. Figure 1 relates these individual skills to an overall pattern or strategy. The example strategy used in the center of this figure is an extension of Polya's (1971) four-step strategy: Define, Plan, Do It, Look Back.

Researchers have learned much about the problem-solving process. For example, we know that we cannot separate the acquisition of knowledge or learning from problem solving. The misconceptions that students have about discipline-specific concepts have been documented. The difficulties of the so-called novices or poor problem solvers have been identified and contrasted with the skills of the so-called experts or skilled problem solvers. Learning objectives have been created for problem solving. Many programs have been created to develop, teach, and evaluate the acquisition of problem-solving skills. Cognitive psychologists have identified the most challenging task in problem solving as the creation of an internal representation of the problem-solving situation. Indeed, much progress has been made.

This chapter focuses on the implications of the interaction between knowledge acquisition and problem solving. It critiques the options that we might use to teach problem solving, and it makes suggestions about the resources that are available and the actions that we might take to teach problem solving.

Learning, Tacit Knowledge, and Problem Solving

We need knowledge or information in order to solve problems, but how we learn information affects how we solve problems. Poor problem solvers have memorized an unstructured set of facts or ideas. There is no hierarchy to their knowledge. It is not connected by pointer words to everyday experiences. It is not understood in any context. No attempt has been made to discriminate among theories, correlations, fundamental laws, definitions, or examples. No abstractions have been attempted. The conditions under which a rule can be applied have not been memorized. The knowledge is not related to other knowledge outside the boundaries of the course. In contrast, good problem solvers have a carefully developed, organized, hierarchical knowledge structure centered around fundamental principles and abstractions. This structure is complete with pointers, it is dynamically changing, and it includes the conditions of applicability for all concepts.

The second key component of problem-solving skills is so-called tacit knowledge. Good problem solvers use such knowledge intuitively, but when they are asked where the knowledge came from, they often reply, "Experience." For example, if someone calculated the velocity of water pumped in a pipeline to be 500 meters per second (m/s), my experience as a chemical engineer would cause me to question this. I think the number should be in the range between 0.5 and 15 m/s, usually between 1 and 2 m/s. How do I know? Experience. Examples of the types of tacit knowl-

Figure 1. Components in the Problem-Solving Process

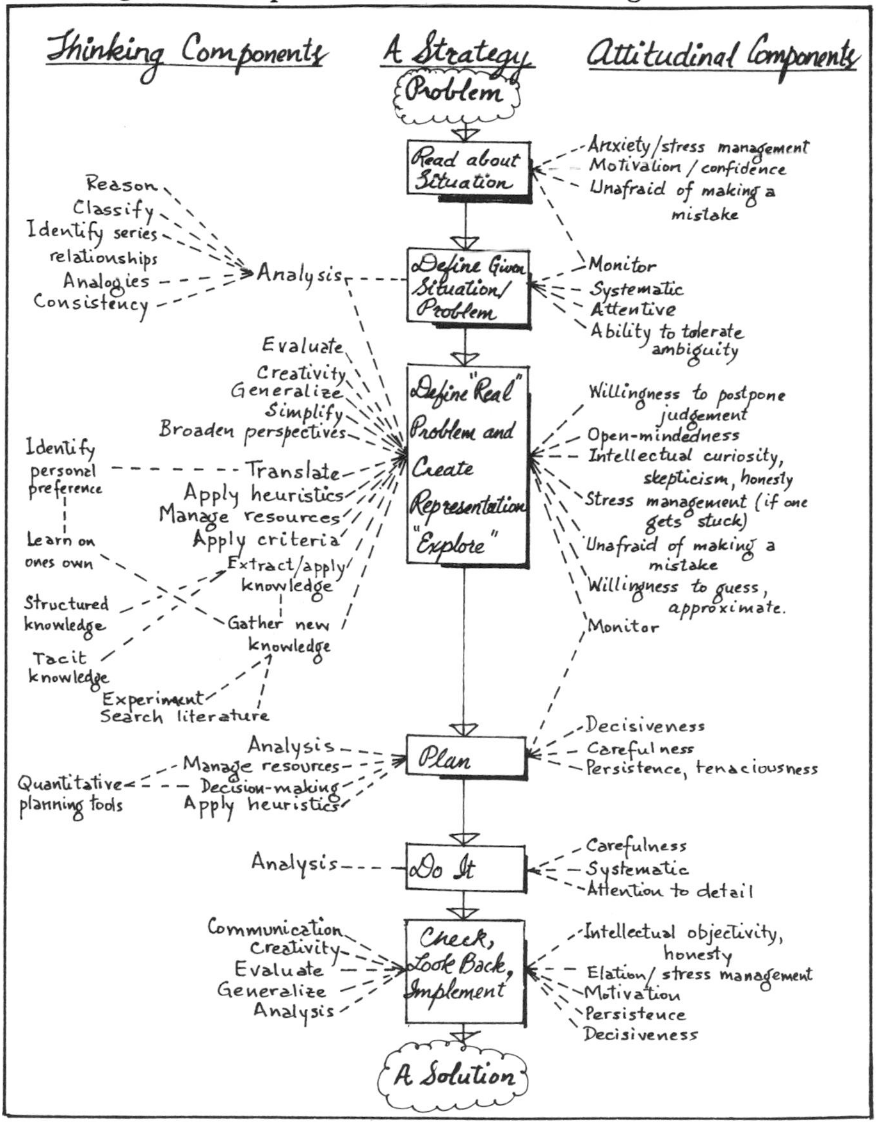

edge that engineers use (and of how one might make the use of such knowledge explicit) are given by Woods (1983b) and by Woods and Kodatsky (1985). Much of the effort spent in developing artificial intelligence systems is devoted to making the expert's tacit knowledge base explicit. Tacit information about problem solving is also included in the knowledge structures of good problem solvers. For example, a problem solver might elect to use an analogy. When asked why, he or she would respond, "Experience." Thus, there is tacit information both in the knowledge domain and in the problem-solving domain. Tacit information from the knowledge domain is essential in the creation of internal representations and in checking and monitoring answers and decisions made during the process.

The third component, problem solving, consists of all the skills defined at the beginning of this chapter. I believe that a domain of knowledge or experience exists that is called *problem solving* and that the application of that knowledge or experience can be taught.

What We Know About the Teaching of Problem Solving

Many find it surprising that books are being written about the teaching of problem solving because they feel that they have been teaching problem solving for years. What is new? They assign homework problems, they work example problems on the board, they require students to use the "design strategy" or the "nursing process" or Polya's (1971) four-step strategy. Besides that, they run a one-hour brainstorming session. What more is there? Perhaps the definition of problem solving given at the start of this chapter may have expanded our perceptions about the subject. But, consider here some other features that research has uncovered about the teaching of problem solving.

First, many students demonstrate that they are excellent at recalling memorized procedures for solving one type of problem. However, recalling memorized procedures is not problem solving; Smith and Good (1985) and Kurlik (1980) call it "exercise solving." Thus, students might be excellent solvers of exercises yet be poor problem solvers. However, both faculty and students rarely distinguish between these two processes, and hence the misconception arises that experience gained by solving many exercises develops skills at solving problems.

Second, to be both effective and transferable, the training in problem solving should be embedded in a subject discipline, not taught as a separate course, and it should include applications to real-world problems.

Third, having students solve many problems and see many worked examples is ineffective in developing problem-solving skill. In a four-year engineering program, students observed professors working more than 1,000 sample problems on the board, solved more than 3,000 assignments for homework, worked problems on the board themselves, and observed faculty demonstrate the process of creating an acceptable internal representation about fifteen times. Yet despite all this activity, they showed negligible improvement in problem-solving skills; the efforts were ineffective (Woods and others, 1985). What they did acquire was a set of memorized procedures for about 3,000 problem situations that they could, with varying degrees of success, recall. If they were given a related but different problem situation, they were not able to bring any new thinking or process skills to bear. Caillot (1983) notes similar findings. Similarly, Meiring (1980) finds that having students solve many "problems" does little to promote problem-solving skill.

Fourth, the types of problems that instructors select are by and large not acceptable media for improving problem solving. Table 1 lists the problems posed over the four-year engineering study just described. The researchers classified each problem according to the level of intellectual activity suggested by Bloom's (1956) Taxonomy. Figure 2 considers the same study from the viewpoint of the appropriateness of the problems that were assigned for the development of different problem-solving skills. In general, most of the problems assigned in the junior and senior years were inappropriate and could not be used to develop the skills.

Fifth, individual differences in learning style, in how information is processed, and in level of cognitive and attitudinal development offer challenges as how best to develop expertise in problem solving (McCaulley and others, 1983). McCaulley addresses some of these issues in Chapter Three.

For all these reasons, we need to ensure that some problems—not exercises—are assigned, that the experience is embedded in a discipline,

Table 1. Types of Problems Posed in a Four-Year Engineering Program

Year	Percentage of program that is required	Number of problems posed Bloom's level				
		Knowledge	Comprehension	Application	Analysis	Synthesis
Freshman	84	1000		5	250	3
Sophomore	100	1000		10	250	2
Junior	82	190		10	85	1
Senior.	69	125		5	8	8
Total		2315		30	593	14

60

Figure 2. Appropriateness of the Usual Assignments to Develop Skills

Explicit problem-solving skill being developed	Ability to use "normal" homework to develop the skill
Awareness of the process used, How to use a strategy How to define the given problem How to extract experience factors Creativity Devising a plan Identifying one's personal Style How to apply heuristics How to identify the structure of knowledge and to learn on one's own Analysis Group skills Listening Interpersonal skills Solving real-world problems Developing one's own style Creating the representation Motivation Working with people	Yes With some difficulty No

that explicit activities—other than the opportunity to work problems—are selected, that the problem media be appropriate for the skills to be developed, and that we account for individual differences—quite a challenge.

Options That Can Be Used To Teach Problem Solving

Many options are used to teach problem solving. To start with, each option is better than doing nothing at all. That is, it is better to give the students 3,000 problems to solve and have them memorize how to do those than it is to give them no problems at all. In this section, we will consider the strengths and weaknesses of the options, and I will supply some examples.

The approaches fall into two overall categories: Some use a holistic approach and consider the process in the context of solving problems completely. For example, ask students to display how they solved problem 4.5 in the text and then reflect on how they did it. Other approaches break the problem-solving process into components, develop each component, and then give practice in applying the relevant skill to the complete problem-solving process. For example, we could focus on creativity, give practice in brainstorming, and, using triggers on the properties of a red brick, embed it in the subject, such as chemical engineering, by brainstorming the possible causes of malfunction in a chemical process, and then we could practice using that skill by solving ordinary homework problems in a concurrent chemical engineering course. Figure 3 contrasts the two approaches. Within each of these two broad categories there are subcategories. For the holistic approach, the subcategories consist of giving the student an opportunity, modeling the process, and facilitating the student's appreciation of the process. For the component approach, the subcategories consist of giving the students an opportunity, providing them with explicit practice on the component, enriching the explicit practice by embedding it in the subject domain, and then providing explicit practice in applying the skill in the holistic activity of solving problems.

Holistic Opportunity. The holistic opportunity approach gives the students many problems to solve, corrects their efforts based on the technical answers that they get, and hopes that they acquire skill at solving problems. This approach, although it is better than giving the students no problems at all to solve, does not develop their problem-solving skills. Yet, this approach is used extensively in our educational programs.

Holistic Modeling. There are many variations on the holistic modeling approach. Instructors can show sample solutions on the board, hand out sample solutions, show through case studies how professionals have handled the problem, or have the students work at the board and display for others how they solved the problem. Most of the efforts in this category fail because they focus on the knowledge components used in arriving at a solution, not on the mental process skills needed to solve the problem. For example, no explicit descriptions are given of how to draw a diagram. No one describes the five failed attempts to create a representation of the problem to be solved; the students only see the "correct" one. We present and see a very sterile and emasculated version of the mental processes used. Indeed, the necessary amount of detail can rarely be included in sample solutions, given the limitations on the number of pages in a textbook. Even the much-discussed case studies usually fall short of displaying the process. Only the technical details of a large, open-ended professional problem are displayed. Such a display serves many useful roles; rarely does it improve problem-solving skill. Furthermore, faculty have great difficulty displaying the process because all the situations with which they

Figure 3. Options for Teaching Problem Solving

Holistic approach	Component approach

Holistic approach:

Problem → Read about Situation → Define Given Situation/Problem → Define "Real" Problem and Create Representation → Plan → Do It → Check, Look Back, Implement → A Solution

Model, monitor, reflect, guide as students do the complete task.

Component approach:

Extract one skill

Develop skill in general context on carefully selected situations that are independent of discipline or subject.

Apply skill in all non-selected situations whenever the skill is needed.

Apply skill in a discipline-specific subject by means of carefully selected situations; for example in Chemistry or Nursing.

work are "exercises" to them. They display how they solve exercises; the students need to see how someone solves problems. Even if faculty could faithfully describe how they have solved problems, their approach may not work for about two thirds of the students because of personal differences in the processing of information. Meiring (1980) points out that teachers always come up with suggestions that work and that move toward a reasonable solution. Thus, students do not see the teacher's frustration, mistakes, or false moves. According to Meiring (1980, p. 33), "The positive effect on a student's problem-solving expertise in merely observing the solutions of other problem solvers is nebulous at best." Having students work problems on the board makes it more probable that "problem solving" instead of "exercise solving" will be displayed. Yet, unless students receive training in how to display the process, only the tip of the iceberg will be shown.

Holistic Facilitation. The holistic facilitation approach asks the students to display the full process either by working at the board or by projecting it via overhead projectors. Then the teacher facilitates an exploration of the processes used. Faculty ask questions to help students clarify their thinking rather than to help them to see how to arrive at an answer. We need to give students time to think about the questions that we pose. In the activity, we should try to involve all the students in the problem-solving process so that we do not have designated problem solvers on the one hand and watchers on the other. Examples of the use of this approach can be found in some of the experiential programs and in some of the problem-based learning programs. Harrisberger and others (1976), Boud (1985), and Barrows and Tamblyn (1980) provide descriptions of such programs.

Component Opportunity. Under the component opportunity approach, we isolate the component, create appropriate "problems," and give students an opportunity to solve them. Some of the components needed to solve problems were identified earlier in this chapter. A number of authors have provided useful resources for different problem-solving skills: for hypothesis generation, Huck and Sandler (1979); for critical reasoning (in biology), Donovan and Allen (1983); for creativity, Raudsepp and Hough (1977); for applying heuristics, the *Lane County Math Program* (1984) and *TOPS (Techniques of Problem Solving)* (1976); for many problem solving skills, deBono, (1983). These are all great resource materials. However, they vary greatly in the degree to which they tell you how to do the task. Most give little or no guidance in that respect. It is up to the reader to analyze the mental skill, discover the process used, and enrich the opportunity by facilitating the student's acquisition of the skill. In contrast, Feuerstein (1985) shows great care in training the teacher to play the facilitation role.

Explicit Prescriptions of Steps to Follow. Some people tackle the teaching of problem solving by identifying and drilling students on the steps that they need to follow in solving problems. Such efforts are embedded in the discipline, but they are usually so specific that they cannot be used to solve other types of problems. An example of an effort in the broader problem-solving context is Sanderson's (1981) collection of questions to ask for thirty-seven different solutions. Such approaches focus only on the strategy component of problem solving, and, if they are deeply embedded in a discipline, they are difficult to transfer.

Explicit Training in Component Skills. Under one variation of the component approach, the skill is isolated, the background psychological fundamentals are given, some objectives are identified, activities aimed at developing the skill are devised, and evaluation procedures are used to help students see whether they have acquired the skill. The medium and the context used in this development are independent of content. Most developers of materials in this field find that the teaching of thinking is so challenging that we must start first with humorous, nonthreatening exercises. Self-performance evaluation is often used. Whimbey and Lochhead (1980, 1984) fall into this class.

Explicit Development and Embedding of Component Skills. Once a skill has been developed in a general context, we can embed the same activities in discipline-specific exercises. For example, after nursing students have completed some Whimbey-Lochhead materials on verbal reasoning (such as, "Indicate the position of the letter in the word 'enrage' that is the seventh letter in the alphabet: a) first, b) second, c) third, d) fourth, e) fifth, f) sixth, g) seventh, or h) eighth"), then we might pose an analogous problem in the context of nursing. The second exercise should require the same processing skills as the first. However, the content should be related to the students' discipline. An example prepared for nurses might be: "A patient has a hematocrit of 0.60. Which of the following evidence is consistent with that information? a) pale complexion, b) heart rate of 110, c) chronic cough, d) normal readings on all vital signs, e) mopping his or her brow, f) nicotine stains on the first two digits of the left hand, g) complaint of dizziness, h) breathing is slow and deep, i) pupils are slow to respond to bright light, j) other." Probably this example would not be understood by anyone not in the nursing field. When this particular example was used in nursing classes, the results indicated that many students had not memorized a reasonable value of the hematocrit. This pointed out their deficiencies in acquiring tacit knowledge. The point is that the student should be asked to draw on his or her expertise in the discipline and be able to consciously follow the thinking process used, as was done in the discipline-independent exercises.

For examples of materials that embed skills developed in a discipline-independent context in a subject discipline, we can point to the HELP (P) materials developed in freshman physics laboratories (Black, 1980), Bauman's (1977) materials in mathematics, and Armitage's (1985) extension of Guided Design materials in accounting. Sparks (1984) has a program in creativity that is embedded in chemical and biomedical engineering.

Explicit Development, Embedding, and Transfer of Component Skills. Under the final variation of the component approach, a skill is isolated. Students practice applying the skill in domain-independent contexts. Then they repeat this practice in domain-specific activities. Finally, they practice applying the skill in the general problem-solving arena. For example, in the topic of stress management, the heuristic of identifying what you have control over is developed first in the context of a paper exercise describing an imaginary examination situation. This development is embedded in a repeat activity in a chemical engineering troubleshooting situation. Then students document their use of this heuristic when they need to and use it during daily problem solving and in day-to-day living experiences. Thus, three distinct activities are developed: isolation and explicit skill development; further development in the subject domain on carefully selected exercises and activities; and transference, integration, and application of the skill in the subject domain on any problem situation and activity that is encountered. The Alverno College program in science, humanities, business, and nursing (Mentkowski and Doherty, 1984) exemplifies this approach. The Kepner-Tregoe approach for the development of decision-making skills might also be classed in this category (Kepner and Tregoe, 1976; Arnold, 1978).

Summary. Many options are available. The holistic approach has been used extensively in the past, but it suffers because it addresses such a host of skills simultaneously that it is hard for both student and teacher to monitor growth. The recent surge of interest in the development of problem-solving skills has tended to isolate and explicitly develop skills, but these suffer unless sufficient care is taken to embed the application in the discipline and to transfer it to the whole task of solving problems. My interpretation of the research literature and developments over the past fifteen years is that our preferred options have been built up in the sequence presented in this section. In other words, we should try to move from giving students the opportunity to solve problems toward the option of explicit development, embedding, and transfer. We start at whichever location we find ourselves and gradually move toward the next level.

So, What Can I Do?

We can do much to help our students improve their problem-solving skills. First, we can help them to see the structure of the knowledge in the discipline. Next, we can identify the tacit knowledge in our subject; the students should integrate this into their knowledge base. Last, we can teach problem-solving skills.

Help Students to See the Structure in Our Discipline. First, we should help students to see that they should take charge of their own learning. Our role is to help them, but it is a team effort. We can help them to identify global perspectives about the subject and provide advance organizers that give the big picture. Undoubtedly, we are doing that now. In addition, however, we can include explicit activities to help them acquire the desired hierarchical structure that is embedded in fundamentals. Suggestions and references for these are given by Woods (1986). From one perspective, we can regard this activity as facilitating "good learning." The research in problem solving has shown that having "good learning" is vital to effective problem solving.

Require Students to Memorize the Tacit Knowledge. What a challenge it is for a chemist to try to explain why a possible reaction is improbable. The experience gathered over many years is used in making the decision. Yet, surely there is something we can do for our students to facilitate the acquisition of such important information. And, important it is, because without it we have trouble creating internal representations, selecting "reasonable" assumptions, and deciding whether an answer sounds reasonable. For suggestions on how to identify, quantify, and assist students in assimilating tacit experience, see Black (1980) for physics and Boud and Gray (1978) and Woods and Kodatsky (1985) for engineering.

Focus on Problem Solving as a Skill to Be Taught. Problem solving is a body of knowledge embedded in cognitive and behavioral psychology that can and should be taught. It has fundamentals, such as those described earlier. People have misconceptions about it; a list is given by Woods (1984). In some sections of the subject, many concepts have been developed—the mathematics of decision making, our knowledge of organizational behavior, the characteristics of effective groups. Our understanding of the skills and domain that we are working with—problem solving— is evolving gradually; we do not have all the answers yet. Nevertheless, I have found that it helps to think of problem solving as a discipline that has its own knowledge structures and its own tacit information.

The first step is to accept the idea that problem solving is a knowledge structure that can be taught, to reflect on the problem-solving activities that we include in our courses, and to sensitize our students to the opportunities that will be used explicitly to explore this subject. This could mean that we might want to grade one assignment for the process, not for the final answer. The greatest challenge for us as educators is not to be too ambitious. These are challenging skills to put in place. They take patience.

Increase Our Students' Awareness of the Processes That They Use. Before we can make much progress in developing problem-solving skills, our students need to be aware of the mental processes that they use, and they need to be able to describe those processes to others. We cannot progress far if we ask, What have you done so far? or Where are you in the problem-solving process? and the student can only respond, "I don't know; it just happens."

To achieve the objective of being aware of the processes, I recommend use of the Whimbey pairs technique and use of some of the exercises developed by Whimbey and Lochhead (1980, 1984). Woods (1984) describes a workshop approach. Many variations can be built on this activity. Stice (1982) gives an example. Other chapters in this volume provide details.

Choose an Option and Patiently Move Toward Higher-Level Options. After we have developed the students' awareness, we can identify where we are in the spectrum of options described earlier. We may want to exploit the students' awareness by having them display the process at the board. We may want to identify some explicit skills to be developed.

Next, we can identify some objectives. Just as we set teaching and learning objectives in our science, humanities, and professional courses, so should we set goals when we teach problem solving or mental processing. Goals help us to select the teaching-learning environment, they help us to prepare the evaluation materials, and they help students to see where they are going and what is expected of them. Fifteen years ago, we could not easily have delineated the goals in problem solving. Now, many options are available. Barrows and Tamblyn (1980) list six competency levels of communication, analysis, problem solving, making value judgments, and interpersonal interactions. Woods and others (1979) list eighteen sequential skills and provide detailed levels for each. Finally, Smith (1981) gives an extensive, structured taxonomy. Our task is to use these resources to create some learning objectives related to the development of problem-solving skills and to include these objectives in our course descriptions.

Once we have identified the objectives, we can assimilate the resources, choose the learning activities, and select the evaluation procedures. Knowles (1975) gives some ideas about how to do this. Woods (1983a) provides a general overview about how to add problem-solving components to our programs.

It should be observed of the approach just outlined that we do not search for good problems and then decide how to use them. Rather, we identify the skills that we plan to tackle, the degree of explicitness with which we want to tackle them, and then the steps involved in developing, embedding, and transferring the skills. That is, we select the objectives first and then choose the problems and the environment.

As a start, Meiring (1980) suggests that we try to devote about 15 percent of the time to the explicit teaching of problem solving. To find such time without removing any subject content from the course, he suggests that we carefully set long-range and short-range objectives so that we focus on only a few objectives at any one time. Making such choices will also help us in selecting the problems to use. One way of proceeding is to use fewer problems and exploit them to satisfy both the problem-solving and the subject content goals. As a teacher, we assume the role of facilitator, with the students doing the thinking, making the decisions, and reflecting on what is going on. Another option has been used by Weeks (1985) in an Oakville, Ontario, science high school program; by Anderson (1984) in a chemical engineering program at the University of Florida; and by Landbeck (1985) and colleagues at Griffith University in Nathan, Australia for a computer science and informatics program. These teachers use a few classes or tutorials near the beginning of the term to develop some skills in general terms, then embed and transfer these skills into the discipline during the remainder of the course. The problem-solving activities should not be rushed. To acquire problem-solving skills requires good planning and a careful statement of overall program and individual course goals. To show the students' development, their growth should be evaluated. One approach to such evaluation combines student self-evaluation of performance with a laboratory notebook in which records are kept of three experiences: the knowledge gained through problem-solving workshops, the weekly application of that knowledge to homework assignments in one designated course, and the use of the knowledge to solve everyday problems (Woods and others, 1984). This approach combines techniques suggested by Barrows and Tamblyn (1980), Chamberlain (1979), and Brown (1980).

Summary

Problem solving can be defined as the mental process used to arrive at a "best" answer to an unknown, subject to a set of constraints. The problem represents something that we have not encountered before. This chapter has listed the skills used to accomplish this task. Emphasis was placed on the role of the structure of how we have stored or learned the fundamentals of a given subject and on the role of the tacit information in the subject.

This chapter has outlined some challenges in the selection and use of problems, and it has listed eight options for the teaching of problem solving. These options include giving students the opportunity to solve many problems, facilitating students' exploration of the mental processes used to solve problems, and providing explicit training in the component skills.

In the classroom, we can help students to see the structure of the subject that we are teaching. We can require them to memorize the tacit information of experience in the subject, focus on problem solving as a skill to be taught, use the Whimbey pairs technique to increase students' awareness of the mental processes that they use, and implement activities to develop specific problem-solving skills. A theme that runs throughout this chapter is that we need first to identify the skills that we want to develop and only then create the problems that we use to facilitate that development.

References

Anderson, T. L. Personal communication. Chemical Engineering Department, University of Florida, Gainseville, 1984.

Armitage, H. Personal communication. Accounting Group, University of Waterloo, Ontario, Canada, 1985.

Arnold, J. D. *Make Up Your Mind.* New York: AMACOM, 1978.

Barrows, H. S., and Tamblyn, R. M. *Problem-Based Learning: An Approach to Medical Education.* New York: Springer, 1980.

Bauman, R. P. *The Logic of Mathematics and Science.* Birmingham: Physics Department, University of Alabama, 1977.

Black, P. J. "Learning Skills." In J. L. Lubkin (ed.), *The Teaching of Elementary Problem Solving in Engineering and Related Fields.* Washington, D.C.: American Society for Engineering Education, 1980.

Bloom, B. S. (ed.). *Taxonomy of Educational Objectives. Vol. 1: Cognitive Domain.* New York: McKay, 1956.

Boud, D. (ed.). *Problem-Based Learning in Education for the Professions.* Kensington, Australia: Higher Education Research and Development Society for Australasia, Tertiary Education Research Center, University of New South Wales, 1985.

Boud, D., and Gray, T.G.F. "Cultivation of Professional Engineering Skills: Development of a Tutorial Method." *European Journal of Engineering Education,* 1978, *3,* 117–133.

Brown, J. M. "Learning Skills as an Overlay in Elementary Calculus." In J. L. Lubkin (ed.), *The Teaching of Elementary Problem Solving in Engineering and Related Fields.* Washington, D.C.: American Society for Engineering Education, 1980.

Caillot, M. "Problem-Solving Research in Elementary Electricity at the LIRESPT." *Problem Solving,* 1983, *5* (3), 2.

Chamberlain, J. *Eliminating Your Self-Defeating Behaviors.* Provo, Utah: Brigham Young University Press, 1979.

deBono, E. *deBono's Thinking Course.* London: British Broadcasting Corporation, 1983.

Donovan, M. P., and Allen, R. D. *Analytical Problems in Biology.* Minneapolis: Burgess, 1983.

Feuerstein, R. *Instrumental Enrichment.* Baltimore, Md.: University Park Press, 1985.

Harrisberger, L., and others. *Experiential Learning in Engineering Education.* Washington, D.C.: American Society for Engineering Education, 1976.

Huck, S. W., and Sandler, H. M. *Rival Hypotheses.* New York: Harper & Row, 1979.

Kepner, C. H., and Tregoe, B. B. *The Rational Manager.* Princeton, N.J.: Kepner-Tregoe, 1976.

Knowles, M. *Self-Directed Learning.* Chicago: Follett, 1975.

Kurlik, S. "Problem Solving in School Mathematics." In *1980 Yearbook of the National Conference of Teachers of Mathematics.* Reston, Va.: National Conference of Teachers of Mathematics, 1980.

Landbeck, R. Personal communication. Griffith University, Nathan, Queensland, Australia, 1985.

Lane County Math Program. Palo Alto, Calif.: Dale Seymour Publications, 1984.

McCaulley, M. H., Godleski, E. S., Yokomoto, C. F., Harrisberger, L., and Sloan, E. D. "Applications of Psychological Type in Engineering Education." *Engineering Education*, 1983, *73*, 394–400.

Meiring, S. P. *Problem Solving: A Basic Mathematics Goal.* Palo Alto, Calif.: Dale Seymour, 1980.

Mentkowski, M., and Doherty, A. "Abilities That Last a Lifetime: Outcomes of the Alverno Experience." *American Association for Higher Education Bulletin*, 1984, *36*, 5–14.

Polya, G. *How to Solve It.* Princeton, N.J.: Princeton University Press, 1971.

Raudsepp, E., and Hough, G. P., Jr. *Creative Growth Games.* New York: Harcourt Brace Jovanovich, 1977.

Sanderson, M. *What's the Problem Here?* Englewood Cliffs, N.J.: Prentice-Hall, 1981.

Smith, M. U., and Good, R. "A Proposed Developmental Sequence for Problem-Solving Ability in Classical Genetics: The Trial-and-Error to Deductive Logic Continuum." Paper presented at the 1985 National Science Teacher's Association Annual Meeting, Cincinnati, April 1985.

Smith, P. *The Development of a Taxonomy of the Life Skills Required to Become a Balanced, Self-Determined Person.* Ottawa, Ontario: Employment and Immigration, 1981.

Sparks, R. E. "Articles and Ideas." *PS News*, 1984, *35*, 16–18.

Stice, J. E. "Teaching Problem-Solving Skills." *Spectrum*, May 16–17, 1982, p. 16–17.

TOPS (Techniques of Problem Solving). Palo Alto, Calif.: Dale Seymour, 1976.

Weeks, V. Personal communication. Oakville High School, Oakville, Ontario, Canada, 1985.

Whimbey, A., and Lochhead, J. *Problem Solving and Comprehension.* Philadephia: Franklin Institute Press, 1980.

Whimbey, A., and Lochhead, J. *Beyond Problem Solving and Comprehension.* Philadephia: Franklin Institute Press, 1984.

Woods, D. R. "Introducing Explicit Training in Problem Solving into Our Courses." *Higher Education Research and Development*, 1983a, *2* (1), 79–102.

Woods, D. R. "Introducing Tacit Information." *Problem Solving*, 1983b, *5*, p. 1.

Woods, D. R. "PS Corner." *Journal of College Science Teaching*, 1984, *13* (6), 467–472.

Woods, D. R. "Skills for Problem Solving." Hamilton, Ontario: Department of Chemical Engineering, McMaster University, 1986.

Woods, D. R., Crowe, C. M., Hoffman, T. W., and Wright, J. D. "Teaching Problem-Solving Skills." In L. P. Grayson and J. M. Biedenbach (eds.), *Proceedings of the Ninth Annual Frontiers in Education Conference.* Washington, D.C.: The Institute of Electrical and Electronics Engineers, and the American Society for Engineering Education, 1979.

Woods, D. R., Crowe, C. M., Hoffman, T. W., and Wright, J. D. "Fifty-Six Challenges to Teaching Problem-Solving Skills." *Chem 13 News.* Waterloo, Ontario: University of Waterloo, 1985, *155*.

Woods, D. R., Crowe, C. M., Taylor, P. T., and Wood, P. E. "The MPS Program." In L. P. Grayson and J. M. Biedenbach (eds.), *Proceedings of the 92nd Annual Conference of the American Society for Engineering Education, Volume 3.* Washington, D.C.: American Society for Engineering Education, 1984.

Woods, D. R., and Kodatsky, W. F. "Discovering Short Cut Methods of Equipment Sizing and Selection." In L. P. Grayson and J. M. Biedenbach (eds.), *Proceedings of the 93rd Annual Conference of the American Society for Engineering Education, Volume 1.* Washington, D.C.: American Society for Engineering Education, 1985.

Donald R. Woods is professor of chemical engineering at McMaster University, Hamilton, Ontario. A developer of the McMaster Problem-Solving Program, he is editor of the column titled "PS Corner" in the Journal of College Science Teaching.

The TAPPS technique is a useful device for the teaching of problem solving because it causes learners to pay attention to basic reasoning skills.

Teaching Analytical Reasoning Through Thinking Aloud Pair Problem Solving

Jack Lochhead, Arthur Whimbey

When teachers are asked to define thinking, most respond with examples of relatively complex mental activity. Often, they refer to rather specialized techniques from specific academic disciplines—perhaps the ability to solve problems that require the use of free body diagrams in determining the dynamics of a system (Reif and Heller, 1984). Alternatively, they may cite general but sophisticated skills, such as Polya's (1971) heuristics. These include such apparently easy activities as thinking of a simpler case or breaking the problem into parts. Unfortunately, problems can be broken into parts or simplified in many ways that are no help at all, and it takes considerable experience and skill to find a useful decomposition.

Cognitive scientists who have studied the differences between the thinking of novices and the thinking of experts say that expert thinking has four main characteristics (Larkin, 1977). First, the expert assembles information from the problem. That is, he or she reads the original statement of the problem, makes a sketch of the situation, visualizes the situation, figures out the meanings of the terms used in the problem statement, and determines the quantitative relation that he or she is asked to find. Next, the expert plans the problem solution. That is, he or she seems to

J. E. Stice (ed.). *Developing Critical Thinking and Problem-Solving Abilities.*
New Directions for Teaching and Learning, no. 30. San Francisco: Jossey-Bass, Summer 1987.

construct qualitative relations between major things happening in the problem. Third, the expert solves the problem. That is, he or she applies principles to generate quantitative equations that he or she then combines mathematically to yield the desired relations. According to the model, this work is a quantitative elaboration of the qualitative relations constructed during planning. Last, the expert checks the solution. That is, he or she reviews the work, using a variety of techniques to check its adequacy.

Unfortunately, classroom teachers who try to encourage their students to employ such habits have generally been disappointed with the results. There is a good reason for this. Recent studies of cognitive processes strongly suggest that expertise in problem solving takes approximately ten years to acquire and that expert reasoning patterns learned in one area do not transfer easily to other areas (Hayes, 1981). Thus, we cannot expect measurable results in the time frames normally available in conventional instruction.

Does this mean that thinking cannot be taught? Common sense suggests that such a conclusion is unsound. We have all learned thinking skills that have helped us to solve problems in areas that differed significantly from the context in which the skills were learned. While it may take at least ten years to acquire expertise in a specific topic, we know that some students are better learners than others from the very beginning. It is a self-evident truth that all novices are not created equal. Some people are far more effective than others in dealing with novel situations.

What is behind this apparent paradox? Why have both research and experienced teachers failed to find skills that lead to better thinking, learning, and problem solving when it seems obvious that such skills exist? In our view, the problem stems from an inappropriate definition of thinking skills. In fact, when one considers how thinking skills are normally identified, it is easy to see why they are likely to be at the wrong level for the purposes of instruction. Polya (1971) defined his thinking skills by introspecting on the things that seemed to be most important to his own thinking. There is no reason to assume that the techniques used by a top-notch mathematician are the skills that distinguish good thinkers from weak reasoners. The cognitive psychologists were a bit more careful, but they nonetheless selected a peculiar problem. In their traditional expert-novice studies, they defined the novice as a student with high grades in an introductory course. This definition was chosen to enable psychologists to study the differences between the expert and the pre-expert by controlling such variables as intelligence and attitude. But, we already know that it takes years of study in a discipline to produce an expert. Thus, the traditional expert–novice study has deliberately selected those aspects of thinking that take ten years to learn.

In order to identify the aspects of thinking that may be susceptible to relatively rapid change, we need to make a different comparison. Such a comparison was made by Bloom and Broder (1950) when they studied successful and unsuccessful student problem solvers at the University of Chicago. They identified aspects of thinking that differ considerably from those listed earlier. Bloom and Broder grouped these aspects under four general headings: understanding of the nature of the problem, understanding of the ideas contained in the problem, general approach to the solution of problems, and attitude toward the solution of problems. Bloom and Broder found that the relevant skills not only were teachable but that such instruction led directly to improved academic performance.

We have produced (Whimbey and Lochhead, 1982) a checklist for students to use in analyzing their own errors. This checklist is reproduced in Exhibit 1. The items on this list are much less sophisticated than those listed earlier, and they are often assumed to be part of every student's repertoire. But, this is precisely the level at which instructional intervention can make a difference. In this chapter, we will pay special attention to the last item on the list, thinking aloud. The expression *thinking aloud* refers to a technique that is becoming increasingly popular within thinking skills programs (Resnick, 1986). There appears to be more agreement that it is useful than there is on why it works. Clearly, thinking aloud helps to communicate thought patterns. Some people refer to the importance of social interaction in the construction of knowledge. They point out that few experts develop or work in isolation. Others point to the need for a thinker to be aware of his or her own thought processes—what Dewey (1933) called *reflective thinking*.

Thinking Aloud Pair Problem Solving

This chapter describes one method for developing the types of thinking skill just discussed and illustrates its application in a variety of disciplines. Of course, there are many other ways of teaching such skills, but the technique that we suggest and its many variants have proved effective in a wide range of circumstances. In Thinking Aloud Pair Problem Solving (TAPPS), two students work cooperatively on a collection of short problems. Each student has a definite role, and it is important for the teacher to insist on strict adherence to some procedural rules. One student is the problem solver. He or she must first read the problem aloud and then continue to talk aloud as much as he or she possibly can about everything that goes on inside his or her head as he or she solves the problem. The other student is the listener. Contrary to expectations, this is by far the more difficult role. First, the listener must make sure that the problem solver keeps talking. Even the shortest silence should be met with "Tell me what you are thinking." However, the listener must do a great deal more. The listener's primary objective is to understand in detail every step and every diversion or error made by the problem solver. A good listener

Exhibit 1. Checklist for Problem Solving

Following is a checklist of sources and types of errors in problem solving. Some of the items overlap, referring to different aspects of the same fault in working problems, but this overlap is unavoidable because the various factors that underlie problem-solving skill are interrelated. Read the checklist aloud, discussing any items that are unclear. Then, as you solve problems, be careful not to make these errors. If you recognize some particular error to which you are especially prone, take extra pains to guard against it. Also, when you are listening to another student solve a problem, watch his approach for errors of the type listed below.

Inaccuracy in Reading

1. Student read the material without concentrating strongly on its meaning. He was not careful about whether he understood it fully. He read sections without realizing that his understanding was vague. He did not constantly ask himself, Do I understand that completely? This showed up in errors he made later.
2. Student read the material too rapidly at the expense of full comprehension.
3. Student missed one or more words (or misread one or more words) because he did not read the material carefully enough.
4. Student missed or lost one or more facts or ideas because he did not read the material carefully enough.
5. Student did not spend enough time rereading a difficult section to clarify its meaning completely.

Inaccuracy in Thinking

6. Student did not constantly place a high premium on accuracy. He did not place accuracy above all other considerations, such as speed or ease of obtaining an answer.
7. Student was not sufficiently careful performing some operation (such as counting letters) or observing some fact (such as which of several figures was the tallest).
8. Student was not consistent in the way he interpreted words or performed operations.
9. Student was uncertain about the correctness of some answer or conclusion but did not check it.
10. Student was uncertain about whether a formula or procedure he used to solve the problem was really appropriate but did not check it.
11. Student worked too rapidly, which produced errors.

12. Student was inaccurate in visualizing a description or a relationship described in the text.
13. Student drew a conclusion in the middle of the problem without sufficient thought.

Weakness in Problem Analysis; Inactiveness

14. Student did not break a complex problem into parts. He did not begin with a part of the problem that he could handle in order to get a foothold. He did not proceed from one small step to the next small step, being extremely accurate with each one. He did not use the parts of the material he could understand to figure out the more difficult parts. He did not clarify his thoughts on the parts that he did understand and then work from there.
15. Student did not draw upon prior knowledge and experience to make sense of ideas that were unclear. He did not try to relate the written text to real, concrete events in making the meaning clear and understandable.
16. Student skipped unfamiliar words or phrases or was satisfied with only a vague understanding of them, rather than trying to obtain a good understanding from the context and the remainder of the material.
17. Student did not translate an unclear word or phrase into his own words.
18. Student did not use the dictionary when necessary.
19. Student did not actively construct (mentally or on paper) a representation of ideas described in the text where such a representation could have helped in understanding the material.
20. Student did not evaluate a solution or interpretation in terms of its reasonableness, that is, in terms of his prior knowledge about the topic.

Exhibit 1. *(continued)*

Lack of Perseverance

21. Student made little attempt to solve the problem through reasoning because he lacked confidence in his ability to deal with this type of problem. He took the attitude that reasoning would not work with this problem. He felt confused by the problem, so he didn't start systematically by clarifying the portions of the problem that were readily understandable and then attempting to work from there.

22. Student chose an answer based on only a superficial consideration of the problem—on an impression or feeling about what might be correct. Student made only a superficial attempt to reason the problem, then guessed at an answer.
23. Student solved the problem in a mechanical manner without very much thought.
24. Student reasoned the problem part way through, then gave up and jumped to a conclusion.

Failure to Think Aloud

The preceding items apply to all academic problem solving. The last item refers specifically to the procedure used in this course.

25. Student did not vocalize his thinking in sufficient detail as he worked through the problem. At places, he stopped and thought without vocalizing his thoughts. He performed a numerical computation or drew a conclusion without vocalizing or explaining the steps that he took.

should not only know the route taken by the problem solver but also understand the reasoning used to select that path, no matter how unreasonable it may be. This means that the listener should ask questions whenever the problem solver's actions become the least bit mysterious. Listeners must avoid solving the problem themselves, and they should avoid asking questions whose real intent is to guide the problem solver. When this technique is used with weak students who are apt to make careless errors, the listener should be instructed to point out that such an error has been made but not state directly what the error is. With more advanced students, it is usually better to let the problem solvers find the error on their own. After each problem, the two students should switch roles but never within a problem.

The teacher's role in the first few classes where the technique is employed should be restricted to rule enforcement. This usually means sitting with a pair of students, monitoring their activity, and paying particular attention to the listener. It is also useful to emphasize to the problem solver that getting the right answer is not as important as verbalizing the route that he or she uses to get to the answer. If we reach an incorrect conclusion but we understand how and why we have reached it, it is far less likely that we will make the error again. After the students have mastered the basic technique, the teacher can provide a variety of support and coaching, but in general the teacher should be more like the listener than the problem solver.

In the remainder of this chapter we will consider a few specific examples of how thinking skills can be taught effectively within the traditional curriculum. We have deliberately selected topics that often prove difficult for a significant fraction of students.

Teaching Analytical Reasoning in Reading Classes

Here is an example of a type of reading selection with which many high school and college students have difficulty (Whimbey, 1983):

> Prior to 1940, overland transportation in Honduras was poorly developed. In 1870, the government had attempted to build a railroad system throughout Honduras. However, primarily due to bad planning and mismanagement of funds, only 88 miles (142 kilometers) of track were actually completed. Later, the banana companies built some 650 miles (1,050 kilometers) of track, but this track was used mainly by those companies and only infrequently by private citizens.
>
> The rest of Honduras was forced to travel overland primarily by way of mule trails until, in the late 1940s, a formal program of road building was begun. As an initial step, the United States helped to finance the construction of the Pan American Highway along the Pacific coast of Honduras. Then, during the 1950s, another highway was built connecting the Pan American Highway to Tegucigalpa. The first large-scale effort to improve the road system in all parts of Honduras came during the late 1960s and early 1970s. The total amount of road length was increased from 1,000 miles (1,600 kilometers) in 1965 to 4,100 miles (6,600 kilometers) in 1975.
>
> 1. Below are three possible titles for this passage. In each blank, write the letter of the phrase (A, B, or C) that best describes that title.
>   ____ Railroad Transportation in Honduras
>   ____ Land Transportation in Honduras
>   ____ Land, Air, and Water Transportation in Honduras
>   (A) too broad (B) too narrow (C) comprehensive title
> 2. How much highway was constructed between the mid 1960s and the mid 1970s?
>   (A) 1,000 miles   (B) 650 miles
>   (C) 3,100 miles   (D) 4,100 miles

Nonanalytical students often say that *Railroad Transportation in Honduras* is the comprehensive title, because railroads are discussed prominently in the first paragraph, and they select their answer on the basis of this dominant impression. Their thinking is one-shot and imprecise. They do not appreciate that the expression *Land Transportation* refers to all types of vehicles traveling on land, and since the passage discusses highways (which means cars) and mule trails in addition to railroads, the title *Land Transportation in Honduras* covers the passage best.

The same type of thinking is often exhibited in answers to the second question. To answer the question, a person must construct a picture of highway growth from information presented in the last sentence of the selection. Weak students frequently answer either 1,000 or 4,100 miles, because they do not mentally spell out the fact that there were already 1,000 miles of highway in 1965. The total increased to 4,100 miles in 1975, so the increase between the mid 1960s and mid 1970s is the difference between 4,100 miles and 1,000 miles or 3,100 miles. What is interesting is not the comprehension question itself but that a wrong answer means that the student is unable to follow the writer's description of highway growth. The student has not learned to interpret terms and mentally construct relationships in a step-by-step manner.

Students who score poorly on reading comprehension tests are often placed in remedial reading classes. Unfortunately, many remedial reading classes place the emphasis on increasing reading speed, not on increasing comprehension. Students are told never to move their lips or to subvocalize while reading, to try to read several words with each glance, never to reread, and to work toward a reading speed of more than 500 words per minute. However, research shows that good readers do subvocalize, that they regularly reread difficult material, that they read basically one word at a time, and that they generally read at a rate of 300 words per minute or less (Whimbey, 1975).

With the recent growth of interest among educators in the teaching of thinking, reading courses are beginning to focus more on comprehension than on speed. A number of classes have started using TAPPS to help students to strengthen their analytical skills in comprehension. For short verbal exercises (two examples are shown later in this chapter), students take turns reading and thinking aloud. For longer exercises in which several paragraphs must be read and a number of questions must be answered, the partners read the selection and answer the questions independently. Then they compare answers and, where the answers differ, defend them, pinpointing the information and reasoning that they used. Teachers report that students initially ask the instructor to settle disputes and provide "right" answers. If the instructor refuses, insisting that the students must justify their own answers, the students gradually learn to read more accurately, and this process is reflected in improved test scores and course work. Results in one exemplary program, Project SOAR at Xavier University, are described later in this chapter.

Another approach to the improvement of analytical reading centers on the development of effective training materials. Normally, when a student reads a selection, the accuracy of the student's comprehension is not monitored sentence by sentence. Weak readers pass through a reading selection without mentally reconstructing the full meaning, but the inaccuracy of their comprehension becomes evident when they try to answer questions at the end. Research on learning has shown that performance without quick feedback does not promote skill improvement. As a remedy, special sets of exercises have been developed, such as the following two, one from near the beginning, one from near the end of a fifty-item series (Whimbey, 1983).

Atlanta has a larger population than Birmingham but a smaller population than Chicago. Write the names of the three cities in order on the diagram.

larger population

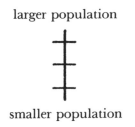

smaller population

In geology, the last 11,000 years are called the *Recent epoch,* and the Recent epoch together with the Pleistocene epoch make up the Quaternary period. Moreover, the Quaternary period together with the Tertiary period make up the Cenozoic era. The Cenozoic is the only era in which periods have been broken down into epochs. The other eras are subdivided only into periods. The era immediately preceding the Cenozoic is the Mesozoic, during which the Jurassic period represents the age of the dinosaurs, although the giant reptiles appeared before the Jurassic and became extinct later than the Jurassic in the Triassic and the Cretaceous periods, respectively. In the still earlier Paleozoic era, the first sharks and reptiles appeared during the next to last period, the Carboniferous, while in the last period of this era, the Permian, reptiles flourished. Preceding the Carboniferous period was the Devonian, and before that, from earliest to latest, the Cambrian, Ordovician, and Silurian periods. Write the eleven periods in order from earliest to latest on a diagram. Do not write eras or epochs.

These exercises require students to make an entry on a diagram after almost every sentence, so there is a pressing incentive for continually accurate comprehension. Students use TAPPS to work the exercises and thus learn to read increasingly difficult material while spelling out relationships fully.

At a more advanced level, the TAPPS approach can be used to have one student paraphrase a paragraph, while the other student listens and challenges the first student's interpretation. An excellent source of material for such exercises is any intermediate- or advanced-level mathematics textbook. Consider the following paragraph from Thomas (1959, p. 37):

> The instantaneous rate of change of y per unit change in x, $f'(x)$, multiplied by the number of units change in x, dx, gives the change that would be produced in y if the point (x,y) were to move along the tangent line instead of moving along the curve.

A student paraphrase of this paragraph could read as follows: "The instantaneous rate of change—what is that? I guess that is what he is going to define. Change of y (that is, how much the graph goes up or down) per unit change in x, $f'(x)$—what is $f'(x)$? $f'(x)$ is the derivative, which is dy/dx, but that is the change in y over the change in x . . . Ah, I see. He has commas around the $f'(x)$. He means for me to refer to what he just said. Why does he have to make it so confusing? Okay, so I have dy/dx . . . Now, that gets multiplied by the number of units change in x, dx—there he goes again. This gives me the change that would be produced in y if the point (x,y) were to move along—what is all this garbage?— move along the tangent line . . . Tangent, that is what I get when I find the derivative. Ah, I see, it is in the diagram. For a particular change in x, there are two possible changes in y: the one we get if we look at the tangent to the curve and the one we get if we look at the curve itself. Now, what does this have to do with instantaneous rate?"

Of course, practice like this takes up valuable class time, and it is possible only if we insist that students read the parts of the text that are not covered in lectures. No matter how clearly that point is emphasized, there is bound to be some rebellion when the first exam proves the truth of the warning. Such protest seems to be an essential element of any program designed to teach thinking through problem solving. Teachers should worry if it is absent.

Students who have mastered the art of TAPPS paraphrasing can be assigned the task of writing out their thoughts while decoding a complex paragraph. This is a tough assignment, and it usually meets stiff resistance. However, students who master the technique find that it is very helpful. Here is a student's sample thought process protocol from an introductory-level course (Narode and others, 1985):

Problem Statement

Perhaps it seems reasonable that the largest planets in our solar system are neither the closest nor the farthest from the sun. Jupiter and Jupiter's neighbor Saturn are the two largest planets. Moving outward from Saturn, the next two planets are Uranus and Neptune, and they are both a little smaller than Jupiter and Saturn. Pluto, the outermost planet, is dwarfed by Jupiter and Saturn, and it is significantly larger than only one planet, the one that is smallest and closest to the sun, Mercury. Jupiter's inside neighbor, Mars, and the next planet in, Earth, are approximately equal in size to Pluto. Venus, whose orbit is between Mercury and Earth, is also between these planets in size. Which planets are fifth and sixth from the sun?

Student Protocol

Perhaps it seems reasonable that the largest planets in our solar system—I'll read the whole problem through before trying to figure it out. I will start to make a diagram; I've read the first two sentences, and I want to start to put things in order. No, better yet, I will read it through completely before making any notes and then reread it. Okay, I read the problem through, and I will have to start at the beginning again. First, I know that the sun is in the middle. Jupiter and Jupiter's neighbor Saturn are the two largest planets. But I don't know where they are in relation to the sun. *Moving outward from Saturn*—okay, I'll put Saturn down. *The next two planets are Uranus and Neptune* . . . a little smaller than Jupiter and Saturn. But, I don't remember whether the problem said where Jupiter was; I just remember it talked about the size. I'll skim the beginning again. Ah, ha. It says *Jupiter's neighbor Saturn,* so I will put Jupiter down, too, and I know that Pluto is farthest out—I'll always remember that. Okay, it doesn't matter how big the planets are; the problem is which are fifth and sixth from the sun. So, I

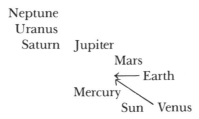

Pluto

Neptune
Uranus
Saturn   Jupiter

Mars
Earth
Mercury
Sun   Venus

will not worry about Pluto's size. *Which is smallest and closest to the sun, Mercury.* Okay, that goes in the diagram now, too. *Jupiter's inside neighbor, Mars*—I'll put Mars in— *and the next planet in, Earth*—okay, that's in there, too, between Mars and Mercury—*are approximately equal*—I won't pay attention to size, I'll just look for the name of another planet in order to finish the diagram and answer the problem. *Venus, whose orbit is between Mercury and Earth.* That's it. I'll put Venus in there, too. But, I better redo the diagram; it is so messy and illegible. The next time, I should just write down the names of the subject asked before making the diagram, so I won't always have to redo it. So, start at the sun, and it's one, two, three, four, five— Saturn—and six—Jupiter.

Pluto
Neptune

Uranus
Saturn—Jupiter
Mars

Earth
Venus
Mercury
Sun

No, that's not right, because they have the same orbit. Or, is that what was said? I'll read the beginning again. So, the problem only said they were *neighbors* and *the two largest planets.* Ah, ha. I've had to reread the entire beginning through midway to find that Jupiter is the closest to the sun in relation to Saturn. So, the diagram is like this:

Pluto
Neptune
Uranus
6 Saturn
5 Jupiter
4 Mars
3 Earth
2 Venus
1 Mercury

Sun

Noticing that we're *moving outward from Saturn* and that Mars is *Jupiter's inside neighbor* helped clarify the problem. Therefore, they are one, two, three, four, five, six: Jupiter is fifth, and Saturn is sixth.

Analytical Reasoning in Mathematics Instruction

Students who have not learned to proceed in accurate, step-by-step fashion when analyzing information are at an extreme disadvantage in trying to master mathematics. For instance, the following problem involves only arithmetic—no algebra, geometry, or calculus. Yet, notice how many mental steps you use in solving it (Whimbey and Lochhead, 1981):

> Four pounds of candy selling at $2 a pound were mixed with two pounds of candy selling at $5 a pound. What was the price per pound of the mixture?

We have found it useful for remedial students to begin with multiple-part problems that elicit the steps necessary to reach an answer. Then the parts are gradually deleted over a series of problems until students go through all the steps on their own. In this way, they learn to engage in a self-initiated step-by-step analysis and solution. Here are two examples from the beginning and middle of such a series (Whimbey and Lochhead, 1981):

1. Bill bought four pounds of candy at $2 a pound. Marlene bought two pounds of candy at $5 a pound.
   a. How much did Bill pay for his candy?
   b. How much did Marlene pay for her candy?
   c. Bill and Marlene combined their candy. How much did it weigh altogether?
   d. How much did the combined candy cost altogether?
   e. How much did the combined candy cost per pound? *Hint:* Divide the total price computed in part d by the total weight computed in part c.
2. Eight gallons of gasoline selling for 55 cents a gallon were mixed with 12 gallons of gasoline selling for 60 cents a gallon.
   a. How many gallons were there in all?
   b. What was the total price for all twenty gallons of the mixture?
   c. What was the price per gallon of the mixture?

Many math teachers find that weak students do not benefit from explanations and illustrations of how complex problems are solved. Just as they miss ideas and come away with incorrect conclusions when reading, they do not follow the explanations of complex solutions. Therefore, rather than placing all the explanations and worked examples at the beginning of the section on a topic, we have increasingly placed complex worked examples throughout a set of problems. Students understand advanced applications of principles better if they have had an opportunity to practice simple cases first. The following ten examples show how worked and unworked problems were interspersed in a set of ninety-seven problems requiring students to translate English into mathematical language (Whimbey and Lochhead, 1981):

1. The combined incomes of Fred and Harry equal $490.
   Mathematical language: $F + H = 490$
2. The combined body weight of Sally, Judy, and Clara is 380 pounds.
   Mathematical language:
3. Cynthia makes as much as Bill and Kathy combined.
   Mathematical language:
4. A man worked for twenty hours at $3 an hour plus ten hours at $5 an hour for a total of $110.
   Mathematical language: $(20)(3) + (10)(5) = 110$
5. Four pounds of candy at $1.20 a pound plus three pounds of better candy at $1.80 a pound cost a total of $10.20.
   Mathematical language:
6. Seven less than three times some number equals 29
   $3n - 7 = 29$ Right
   $7 - 3n = 29$ Wrong: common error
7. Three more than five times some number equals 38.
   Mathematical language:
8. Six less than double some number equals one more than that number.
   Mathematical language:
9. A car drove some number of hours at 50 miles per hour and four less hours at 60 miles per hour for a total of 860 miles.
   Mathematical language: $(n)(50) + (n - 4)(60) = 860$
   $$50n + 60(n - 4) = 860$$
10. A car traveled a certain number of hours at 40 miles per hour and three less than twice that many hours at 50 miles per hour for a total of 410 miles.
    Mathematical language:

These examples are all very elementary. In fact, they come from a remedial-level course. By placing the emphasis on problem solving, we are able to move on to much more demanding tasks even while keeping within a relatively low level of mathematical content. The most sophisticated of these exercises require students to write a detailed account of their thinking while working on what for them are difficult problems.

An even deeper level of understanding is demanded when students are asked to explain their thinking at a level that someone who knew little mathematics could understand. Often, it is useful to insist on the use of diagrams or some other specific representation, as in the following example:

Problem Statement

A flask containing 650 doses of medicine had five milliliters of the medicine removed for experimentation. Because of an emergency, another clinic was sent one fifth of the remainder. Afterward, only 512 doses remained. Calculate the dosage in milliliters. *Hint:* Be careful to recognize that there is a difference between number of doses and number of milliliters per dose.

Student Protocol

I've read the problem a couple of times, and I'm not sure where to start. *A flask containing 650 doses of medicine*—why don't I start by drawing a flask?

650
doses

Here is a full flask,
and it contains 650 doses.

Next, five milliliters are removed. I don't know how much that is in proportion to the 650 doses, so I will just shade in a little bit at the top, which means it has been taken out.

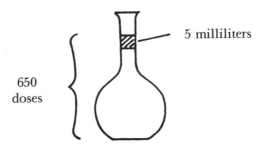

5 milliliters

650
doses

Now, another clinic was sent one fifth of the remainder. That means that I will have to divide what is left in the flask into five equal parts. But, how do I do that? The flask is a funny shape, and if I draw lines to separate it into five parts, I won't be sure that they will be five equal parts. Is there another way I can draw the picture? Does the flask have to look like the kind in the chemistry lab, or can I just use a box to represent 650 doses? I don't see why not. After all, 650 doses is 650 doses—right? I think so.

Okay, I'm starting over again. I'm going to draw a box that represents 650 doses of medicine. And, I'm going to take 5 milliliters out of one corner.

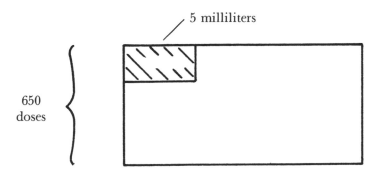

I shaded it to show that it was taken out.

Oh, no. I have the same problem as before. I can't separate the remainder after I take the five milliliters out into five equal parts. I have to do it another way. I will take the five milliliters out of one end.

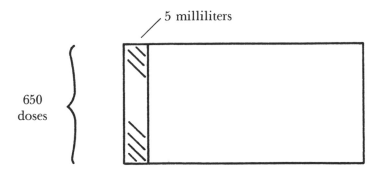

Good. Now I am left with something I can section into five equal parts. I will draw the five equal parts and shade in the portion sent to another clinic, which will mean that it has been taken out.

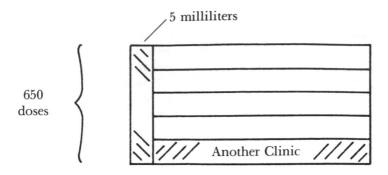

Now, the problem says that only 512 doses remained. That means that there are four equal parts remaining, which total 512 doses. Ah, ha. Then, there are 512/4 = 128 doses in each part. That must also mean that the other clinic was sent 128 doses, since its portion is the same size as each of the other equal parts. I will write this information in my drawing.

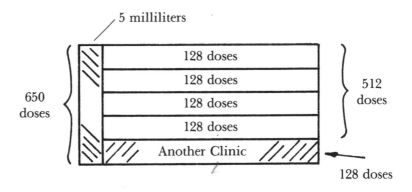

Let me review what the drawing tells me. There are 650 doses total. Five hundred twelve doses are still in the flask, and 128 doses were sent to another clinic. Then 512 + 128 = 640 doses accounted for. What about the five milliliters?

There are 650 doses in all. Six hundred forty of them are accounted for. Then ten remain. Those ten doses must be the five milliliters.

If there are five milliliters in ten doses, how many milliliters are in one dose? This reminds me of one of those miles per gallon problems, only now it is milliliters per dose.

With miles per gallon, I always put the miles on the top and the gallons on the bottom, like this:

$$\frac{\text{miles}}{\text{gallons}}$$

I will set up the milliliters per dose problem the same way:

$$\frac{\text{milliliters}}{\text{dose}} = \frac{5}{10}$$

If that is reduced, it comes to 1/2. That means there is one milliliter for every two doses. So, if there is one milliliter in every two doses, there must be 1/2 milliliter for every one dose.

My answer for this problem is that there is 0.5 milliliter of medicine in every dose of medicine in the flask.

How Much Does Training in Analytical Thinking Improve Academic Performance?

Much more research is needed on the efficacy of teaching analytical reasoning, but a number of programs are beginning to show positive results. One example is Project SOAR (Stress on Analytical Reasoning) at Xavier University in New Orleans, a five-week, prefreshman program that has been conducted for 150 to 200 students a summer for eight summers.

SOAR has two components: specially designed laboratory exercises between 9 A.M. and noon and training in analytical reasoning and reading between 1 and 3 P.M. The laboratory exercises were developed by faculty from the departments of biology, chemistry, mathematics, computer sciences, and physics. Each exercise is organized in a "learning cycle" format (Karplus, 1974) with exploration, invention, and application phases. For the afternoon sessions, students use TAPPS while working reading, math, and reasoning exercises. Exercises begin with easy items like those shown earlier and progress to problems requiring an extended series of self-initiated mental steps, such as the following math word problem (Whimbey and Lochhead, 1984):

One light flashes every two minutes, and another light flashes every seven minutes. If both lights flash at 1 P.M., what is the first time after 3 P.M. on the same day when both lights flash together?

Statistics have been collected to evaluate SOAR's effectiveness. For example, students who initially score below 700 (combined math and verbal) on the Scholastic Aptitude Test (SAT) gain an average of 120 points on the SAT and three grade levels on the Nelson-Denny Reading Test (Hunter and others, 1982). More important to Xavier's faculty than the test score gains is that SOAR participants are twice as likely as other Xavier students to pass their freshman science and math courses (Carmichael, 1982). Further, Xavier's mathematics department has noted a very substantial increase in enrollment in advanced mathematics courses. Analytical training has also been incorporated into a number of premed courses. This development, combined with SOAR, is seen by staff to be a major contributor to the fact that for several years Xavier, a traditionally black college, has placed more black students in medical school than all other colleges in Louisiana combined (Association of American Medical Colleges, 1984).

A recent study by New Jersey's Task Force on Thinking illustrates the importance of the type of analytical reasoning skills that we stress here for basic academic achievement. The subtests of the New Jersey College Basic Skills Placement Test were correlated with our test of analytical reasoning, the Whimbey Analytical Skills Inventory (WASI). The correlations for 513 college freshmen are shown below (Morant and Ulesky, 1984).

Reading Comprehension	Sentence Sense	Computation	Elementary Algebra	Essay
.76	.75	.76	.70	.56

The correlation of .70 between the algebra subtest and the WASI is particularly interesting because the WASI does not contain any algebra problems. Instead, it consists of analytical reasoning items, such as the following (Whimbey and Lochhead, 1982):

Verbal Analogy   From the four possibilities given, choose the pair of words which causes the incomplete sentence to make the most sense. ____ is to *cave* as *car* is to ____ .
(a) stone:steel   (b) primitive:modern
(c) apartment house:horse   (d) modern:primitive

Figural Reasoning   Figures 1 through 4 form a series that changes in a systematic manner according to some rule. Try to discover the rule and choose from among the alternatives the figure that should occur next in the series.

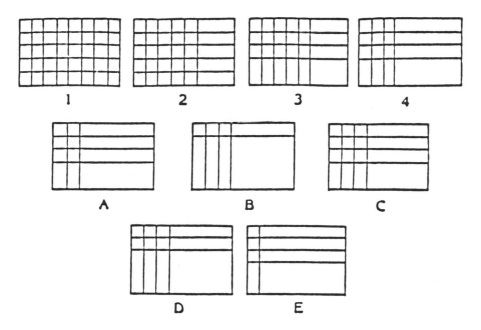

The high correlation between the WASI and the algebra subtest suggests that the mental ability tapped by these reasoning questions is used in mastering and applying algebra. The correlation of .76 between the WASI and the Reading Comprehension subtest is interesting, too, because the WASI does not contain any prose passages followed by comprehension questions, as reading tests do. Apparently the ability tapped by the WASI is also used in comprehending reading selections.

Summary

The teaching of thinking through problem solving has costs as well as benefits. It is widely agreed that one of these costs is content. The time demanded to engage in serious problem solving reduces the number of topics that can be covered in a course. In this chapter we have considered a second cost: the need to pay specific attention to some very basic reasoning skills and thus by implication to delay the introduction of some of the advanced skills. For teachers who gain gratification from demonstrating their own competence, this may be too high a price. But, it is not too high for teachers whose satisfaction come from observing students grow and who have the patience and the curiosity to investigate how their students think. We at least have found that the rewards of teaching basic analytical skills far outweigh the costs.

92

References

Association of American Medical Colleges. *Admission Action Summary Report.* Washington, D.C.: Association of American Medical Colleges, 1984.

Bloom, B. S., and Broder, L. J. *Problem-Solving Processes of College Students: An Exploratory Investigation.* Supplementary Educational Monographs No. 73. Chicago: University of Chicago Press, 1950.

Carmichael, JW, Jr. "Improving Problem-Solving Skills: Minority Students and the Health Professions." In K. V. Lauridsen and C. F. Myers (eds.), *Summer Programs for Underprepared Freshmen.* New Directions in College Learning Assistance, no. 10. San Francisco: Jossey-Bass, 1982.

Dewey, J. *How We Think.* New York: Heath, 1933.

Hayes, J. R. *The Complete Problem Solver.* Hillsdale, N.J.: Erlbaum, 1981.

Hunter, J., Jones, L., Vincent, H., and Carmichael, JW, Jr. "Project SOAR: Teaching Cognitive Skills in a Precollege Program." *Journal of Learning Skills,* 1982, *1*, 24–26.

Karplus, R. *The Science Curriculum Improvement Study.* Berkeley: University of California, 1974.

Larkin, J. H. "Skilled Problem Solving in Physics: A Hierarchical Planning Model." Berkeley: University of California SESAME Technical Report, 1977.

Morant, E., and Ulesky, A. "Assessment of Reasoning Abilities." *Educational Leadership,* 1984, *42*, 71–74.

Narode, R., Schifter, D., and Lochhead, J. *A Course Guide to Math 010L: Fundamental Math Concepts/Problem Solving I.* Amherst: Cognitive Processes Research Group, Department of Physics, University of Massachusetts, 1985.

Polya, G. *How To Solve It: A New Aspect of Mathematical Method.* Princeton, N.J.: Princeton University Press, 1971.

Reif, F., and Heller, J. I. "Prescribing Effective Human Problem-Solving Processes: Problem Description in Physics." *Cognition and Instruction,* 1984, *2*, 117–175.

Resnick, L. B. "Education and Learning to Think." Draft report prepared for the Commission on Behavioral and Social Sciences and Education, National Research Council, 1986.

Thomas, G. B., Jr. *Reading Elements of Calculus and Analytic Geometry.* Reading, Mass.: Addison-Wesley, 1959.

Whimbey, A. *Intelligence Can Be Taught.* New York: Dutton, 1975.

Whimbey, A. *Analytical Reading and Reasoning.* Stamford, Conn.: Innovative Science, 1983.

Whimbey, A., and Lochhead, J. *Developing Mathematical Skills: Computation, Problem Solving, and Basics for Algebra.* New York: McGraw-Hill, 1981.

Whimbey, A., and Lochhead, J. *Problem Solving and Comprehension: A Short Course in Analytical Reasoning.* Philadelphia: Franklin Institute Press, 1982.

Whimbey, A., and Lochhead, J. *Beyond Problem Solving and Comprehension.* Philadelphia: Franklin Institute Press, 1984.

Jack Lochhead is director of the Center for the Study of Cognitive Approaches to Mathematics Instruction, Department of Physics, University of Massachusetts at Amherst.

Arthur Whimbey is an independent educational consultant who currently lives in Lake Worth, Florida.

What are the goals of education? We can teach people a lot,
but if we do not teach them how to use what they know,
we have fallen short of what we all have the potential of
achieving.

Learning How to Think: Being Earnest Is Important, but It's Not Enough

James E. Stice

Many conscientious, hardworking college students pass through an insti-
tution and graduate with added knowledge and with some additional
skills, but they are otherwise not much changed by the experience. Professors, too, earnest and well-intentioned, teach for years without doing anything that differs much from what their professors did before them and
sense vague dissatisfaction with the progress of their students. With apolo-
gies for writing a chapter that is autobiographical, I wish to follow the
thread of my own journey through higher education, a voyage that has
yet to reach its destination.

I was born, grew up, and went to college in Fayetteville, Arkansas.
My grade school and high school preparation were first rate. I made good
grades because I had a good memory and because I was reasonably earnest
about my studies. I enrolled in engineering college in the fall of 1945,
along with a large number of returning GIs from World War II. They had
been out of school for a while, and their math and science skills were
rusty. Mine were fairly shiny, since I had gotten out of high school the
previous June. I made excellent grades the first two years while the veterans were catching up. During my last two undergraduate years, some

J. E. Stice (ed.). *Developing Critical Thinking and Problem-Solving Abilities.*
New Directions for Teaching and Learning, no. 30. San Francisco: Jossey-Bass, Summer 1987.

clouds drifted across my academic horizon. Some of the veterans began to pass me by. I did not do well on some examinations and wondered how my classmates managed to breeze through them. I still used my memory a great deal, and I was more earnest and diligent in my studies, but the results were not as good. I made a few C grades my junior year, and in my senior year I made some more.

The class of 1949 was not burdened with job offers. Two thirds of the senior chemical engineers, including myself, got no offers at all, at least immediately. However, just to be on the safe side I had applied to a couple of graduate schools, and I was accepted. I had lost a lot of my original self-confidence, and I didn't feel that I was ready to go to work in any case.

My first year in graduate school was traumatic. The professors were demanding, and they played by different rules. Tests were often about things that we had not studied. The students were very good, too, industrious and able. My memory was not as helpful as it had been in the past, because there now were a lot of things to remember, but I was very diligent in my studies. If you are having trouble keeping up, you work that much harder doing what has made you successful in the past, right? It didn't help. I recall the second graduate course that I took in thermodynamics very well. The professor gave out a lot of homework, and his problems were tough. He also called the roll every day with a ten-minute pop quiz. Here is a representative problem: "It is snowing. A snowplow starts out at 9:00 A.M. and moves two miles the first hour. After two hours, it has moved three miles. The rate of snowfall is constant, and the speed of the plow is inversely proportional to the depth of the snow. When did it start to snow?" (For a solution to virtually the same problem, see Graham, 1959. The answer to the problem as it is stated here is 8:23 A.M.). *This* was a thermodynamics problem? It wasn't like any of the homework that had been assigned, and we were supposed to solve it in ten minutes. Surely the prof was joking! He wasn't. I made a lot of zeros on those pop quizzes. So did a lot of others, but I didn't know it then. (Years later I realized that my professor had the right idea: Give students problems that differ somewhat from what they have seen, and let them practice their problem-solving skills. The trouble was that he did not give us a strategy to follow, so our practice was not intelligently directed. His classes made my stomach hurt, and many of us learned to hate thermodynamics.)

I began to sense the dark clouds of doom gathering over me and to feel that my career as a graduate student was drawing to a premature and ignominious end. It was, too. I was making too many C's, and C's are not good for graduate students. If something did not change soon, I was not going to get that master's degree. Things did change, however. My roommate, Dick Bukacek, had been observing my troubles, and he undertook to bail me out. We had a number of little coaching sessions in which he brutally and ruthlessly forced me to begin to *think* about some of the concepts that I had been studying. He agreed that the what was important, but he wanted me to pay more attention to the hows and the whys. A sample session might have gone something like this:

> *B:* Derive the equation for the fugacity of liquid component *A* in a binary mixture.
> *S:* I don't remember it.
> *B:* I didn't ask you to write it down, I asked you to derive it.
> *S:* I don't know how.
> *B:* You know all you need to know, just apply what you know.
> *S:* I don't know where to start.
> *B:* Start somewhere.
> *S:* (Beginning to panic) But, Dick, I really don't know where to start. I remember that it involves Gibbs free energy and activity, but I don't know how to put it together.
> *B:* Look, Stice, a lot of your problem is that you know something about Gibbs free energy and something about activity, but you don't understand the concepts. The equations aren't the concepts. It doesn't matter much *where* you start. Start somewhere. You may not get very far at first, but you'll find out pretty quickly what you don't understand. Then we'll get that straightened out, and you'll have learned something. So, you try again, and things will make more sense, and you'll get further. Finally, you'll be able to put it all together, and you'll have a much better feel for this whole vapor-liquid equilibrium business. You know enough to do it. Now, quit your wailing and complaining, and get started, dammit!

You get the idea. Bukacek brushed my alibis aside, made me explain why I did what I did, and never let up on me. After several weeks, it began to be helpful, although it was still painful. I began to understand more of the underlying structure of the science, and my self-confidence began to grow. More and more I could do what he asked of me with only occasional hints from him. My performance in my courses improved, too. I obtained my master's degree, got a job, and went to work in industry. After learning the ropes, I did a pretty good job as a process engineer. Bukacek had started me on the road to analytical thinking. I do not know whether he even remembers these sessions, but they were crucial to my intellectual development. I owe him a great deal. Meanwhile, thirty blocks to the south, Lois Broder was doing her master's thesis with Benjamin Bloom at the University of Chicago. Her topic was the problem-solving processes of college students (Bloom and Broder, 1950).

I never intended to be a teacher but sort of got into the profession through the back door. I found that I enjoyed it hugely and decided to make college teaching my career. It did not take long to see that a lot of my students were like the Jim Stice of 1950. They were bright, hardworking, and ambitious, but they also were memorizers. If you gave them a problem that was a little different from what they had seen before, they were stumped. How could I use Bukacek's methods with a class of thirty students? I lacked the resources and the time. So, I lectured and did what I could to help those who came to see me after class.

Twenty-three years passed, and I learned some things about the craft of teaching. Larry Grayson introduced me to the idea of using instructional objectives, Dwight Scott showed me the wisdom of teaching and testing at higher levels of Bloom's taxonomy (Bloom, 1956), and Fred Keller (1968) convinced me of the value of individualizing and self-pacing instruction. While I was trying out these ideas, which were new to me, others were developing methods of teaching problem solving. Moshe Rubinstein (1975, 1980) first offered his course "Patterns of Problem Solving" at UCLA in the fall of 1969; now 1,200 students take that course every year. Charlie Wales and Bob Stager (Wales and Stager, 1977) conceived of Guided Design and began to teach their ideas at West Virginia University in 1970. Don Woods and others (1975, 1979) at McMaster University were wrestling with the challenges of improving the analytical skills of engineering students, and Woods has been tireless in his efforts to stimulate colleagues to join this movement. Art Whimbey, Jack Lochhead, and others (Whimbey and Lochhead, 1982, 1984) at the University of Massachusetts were doing exciting things in the Cognitive Development Group. The University of Nebraska ADAPT program also got under way in the mid 1970s. I did not know about any of these programs at the time.

In June 1980, I attended the annual conference of the American Society for Engineering Education at the University of Massachusetts at Amherst. One of the preconference workshops was titled "Methods for Teaching Problem Solving," and it was presented by Lois Broder Greenfield, Charlie Wales, Don Woods, and Jack Lochhead. I knew Lois and Charlie, and I decided to attend. We were introduced to Lois's work, to Woods's program, to the Whimbey pairs technique, and to the Wales-Stager Guided Design concept. The discussions made me recall my vague feelings of insecurity as an undergraduate, my trials as a graduate student, my roommate's successful efforts to save my bacon, my fumbling attempts to help my own students, and my frustration at the lack of time and resources and of a very clear idea of how to go about it. I was ready for that workshop, and I lit up like a Schlitz beer sign.

I returned to my own campus and began to use the Whimbey pairs technique in my own classes. The results were encouraging. I didn't "save" every student, but I got subjective evidence that many students left the course with better problem-solving skills than they had when they entered, and they seemed to enjoy the exercises. I read, talked to people, and tinkered with the format. I think Stonewater (1980) is right. He says that the particular method used to teach problem solving is probably not all that important—they all seem to give positive results—but that five features of the various methods that can be used seem to be necessary: First, listen to Piaget. His theory on how the concrete learner leaves the world he perceives through his senses to move into a world of abstractions is absolutely critical for the development of instruction for problem solving. Second, insist on mastery learning of content, but allow learners to get there in their own time. Third, pay attention to the design of instruction. The learning goals set and the methods used to achieve them affect performance. Fourth, give students feedback on the many little details that go into problem solving as well as on their success. Fifth, encourage group learning. Two problem solvers are better than one. In general, an overt attempt by the teacher to teach problem solving focuses attention on it and makes things happen.

In the early 1980s, our center began to study large undergraduate classes at our university, because many classes were getting bigger, and there were more of them. Karron Lewis (Lewis and Woodward, 1984) conducted the study, which was aimed at discovering what worked in large classes (those with a hundred students or more) and what did not work. She worked with nineteen professors, all volunteers, from the colleges of natural sciences, business, engineering, and liberal arts. We decided to try to get some information on which level of Bloom's taxonomy the courses were taught.

The results were interesting. Of the nineteen courses in the study, only five had any work beyond Bloom's level 3 application: an anthropology course, "Nonordinary Reality," that examined the use of hallucinatory drugs in primitive societies; a sociology course, "Sex Roles"; a government course in U.S. and Texas politics; "Introduction to Astronomy"; and a course in U.S. history since the Civil War. Further, the students reported satisfaction with these courses. All five courses were considered tough, but they ranked first, second, third, fifth, and seventh, respectively, in enjoyment. Conventional wisdom has it that students prefer courses that do not make too many demands on them and that students do not give good evaluations to those who teach tough courses. I never believed this particular myth about teaching, because I have seen too many exceptions. The students in those five tough courses evidently did not believe it either.

I have no evidence that undergraduate classes at the University of Texas are much different from those at other colleges and universities; I suspect that the results obtained in the large-class study would be duplicated at many other institutions. Further, I suspect that studies of small classes would produce similar results—a hunch as yet unsupported by data. I have come to feel that much too much time is spent teaching at the knowledge, comprehension, and application levels. Not nearly enough

98

time is spent teaching process—that is, teaching students how to use what they know.

When a statement like this is made to faculty colleagues, they react immediately, often with some heat. They cry with honest anguish that there is already too much to cover in the semester and that their students are going to need to know the latest methods, techniques, theories, or equipment when they graduate and go to work. How can they cover the material and teach problem solving, too? I certainly can sympathize with their feeling, since I felt as they do not long ago. At the same time, I now believe that the horse they are riding wears feathers. Students do not need to know all the new stuff. A lot of things that I learned during the years of my formal education are only of historical interest now. How many electrical engineers use an RCA tube manual now? How many chemical engineers use the Ravenscroft method to design a liquid–liquid extraction battery? How many lab technicians use wet methods to do chemical analyses? Who uses Theory X in management any more? Further, none of us can have any idea of what our students will be doing when they leave school, so we cannot predict which fraction of the curriculum will turn out to be important in their lives. At the same time, it is a safe bet that much of their future will lie in areas that we have not even thought about yet. Finally, people continue to learn after they graduate, and most will have forty years or more in which to master new technology, new ideas, and new techniques.

If we teach our students how to use what they know and how to learn what they will need to know, it seems to me that both the individual and society at large will be better served. If we were to prune the out-of-date and the merely nice-to-know from our courses and teach our courses from a problem-solving perspective, the long-term results would be better. It is true that it takes more time to engage in problem-solving activities in class than it does to lecture on the content; at least that has been my experience. In that case, I suggest that the content be pruned a bit more. I believe that paying more attention to process is worth the sacrifice of some content in our courses.

References

Bloom, B. S. (ed.). *Taxonomy of Educational Objectives.* Vol. 1. *Cognitive Domain.* New York: McKay, 1956.

Bloom, B. S., and Broder, L. J. *Problem Solving Processes of College Students: An Exploratory Investigation.* Supplementary Educational Monographs No. 73. Chicago: University of Chicago Press, 1950.

Graham, L. A. *Ingenious Mathematical Problems and Methods.* New York: Dover, 1959.

Keller, F. S. "Goodbye, Teacher . . ." *Journal of Applied Behavior Analysis,* 1968, *1* (1), 79–89.

Lewis, K. G., and Woodward, P. J. "What Really Happens in Large University Classes?" Paper presented at the American Educational Research Association Meeting, New Orleans, April 23–27, 1984. ED 245 590

Rubinstein, M. F. *Patterns of Problem Solving.* Englewood Cliffs, N.J.: Prentice-Hall, 1975.

Rubinstein, M. F. "The Development of a Problem-Solving Course at UCLA." In L. P. Grayson and J. M. Biedenbach, (eds.), *Proceedings of the Tenth Annual Frontiers in Education Conference.* Washington, D.C.: The Institute of Electrical and Electronics Engineers, Inc., and the American Society for Engineering Education, 1980.

Stonewater, J. K. "Strategies for Problem Solving." In R. E. Young (ed.), *Fostering Critical Thinking.* New Directions for Teaching and Learning, no. 3. San Francisco: Jossey-Bass, 1980.

Wales, C. E., and Stager, R. A. *Guided Design, Part I.* Morgantown: West Virginia University, 1977.

Whimbey, A., and Lochhead, J. *Problem Solving and Comprehension: A Short Course in Analytical Reasoning.* (3rd ed.) Philadelphia: Franklin Institute Press, 1982.

Whimbey, A., and Lochhead, J. *Beyond Problem Solving and Comprehension.* Philadelphia: Franklin Institute Press, 1984.

Woods, D. R., Wright, J. D., Hoffman, T. W., Swartman, R. K., and Doig, I. D., "Teaching Problem-Solving Skills." *Engineering Education,* 1975, *66,* 238–243.

Woods, D. R., and others. "Major Challenges to Teaching Problem-Solving Skills." *Engineering Education,* 1979, *70* (3), 277–284.

James E. Stice is T. Brockett Hudson Professor of Chemical Engineering and director of the Center for Teaching Effectiveness at the University of Texas at Austin.

Lecturing is not a very effective way of teaching analytical skills. The methods that work better focus attention on the defining and development of these skills and then provide intelligent practice. A list of resources is provided.

Further Reflections: Useful Resources

James E. Stice

Much formal instruction down through the centuries has followed the model in which an instructor stands in front of an audience of students or trainees to tell them about things they should know, or understand, or be able to do. Hearing is not a particularly efficient way of learning, especially for those who are not "earminded," and with the advent of paper, pencil, and printing, the learners could take notes and read books. Laboratory courses, which allowed learners to obtain concrete experience with the subjects under study, were a further advance. Audiovisual materials and equipment made it possible to show a whole class a drawing too complicated to reproduce on the chalkboard, a photograph taken through a microscope, or a picture of a particular painting, building, or other artifact. Studies have shown that retention of material learned increases as more of one's senses are involved in the process.

Because lecturers tend to use most of the time available to talk to (or at) a class, students tend to be passive receivers of information. They listen, take notes, and pay varying amounts of attention, depending on their interest in the subject, the lecturer's enthusiasm, and competition from other things on their minds. Research indicates that the average adult can maintain moderate concentration for about twenty-two minutes. Questions or comments from others can sharpen the listener's concentra-

J. E. Stice (ed.). *Developing Critical Thinking and Problem-Solving Abilities.*
New Directions for Teaching and Learning, no. 30. San Francisco: Jossey-Bass, Summer 1987.

tion for brief periods, but in many classes students do not often ask questions, and the incidence of questioning decreases as class size increases. Students often do not do much active processing of the ideas that are presented. They may go over their notes after class to try to make sense of what they heard, to organize and integrate the new material into what they already know, and perhaps to fill in where they missed something. Other students may do very little outside class unless a major exam is approaching.

The lecture method can be useful for teaching facts and concepts and for showing how to apply them in more or less straightforward situations. If lectures are well done, they are an excellent way for a teacher to model professional behavior and to use enthusiasm to motivate the listener to want to know more about the subject. (For many people, seeing a play performed has far more impact than reading the play.) Lecturing is not as useful in teaching at the higher levels of Bloom's taxonomy: analysis, synthesis, and evaluation. Learning theorists tell us that the best way of teaching at these levels is to give students the opportunity to analyze, synthesize, or evaluate on their own. Then they must be given rapid, accurate feedback on their performance. Finally, they need lots of practice to develop their skills. (Nothing more will be said about synthesis and evaluation here, since the subject of this sourcebook is the teaching of problem-solving skills, which I view as a subset of analysis.)

Many teachers seem to feel that people will develop analytical skills if they are given enough practice. However, most teachers do not illuminate the process. At best, they model it. It does not seem to help students very much to see how a teacher analyzes a given situation. They may not follow the strategy, or they may not even be aware that there is a strategy. The strategy that Woods likes to use is Polya's, because it is simple, it is easy to teach, and it makes sense. As modified by Woods, Polya's strategy has five steps: Define the Problem, Think About It, Plan, Carry Out the Plan, and Look Back. Most of us think about example problems, arguments, and criticisms before we present them in class. We make some mistakes, follow some blind alleys, and flail around in the rough before we work things out in our minds. What the students see is the problem definition, followed by the solution—the carrying out of the plan. They do not see the Think About It and the Plan steps, the early fumbles and false starts, the mental twiddling of fingers, the assumptions we made or why we made them. What they see is a production—clean, neat, even elegant! But, that production is the product of a process, and the students see only parts of the process, not the most important parts at that.

Greenfield in Chapter One and Lochhead and Whimbey in Chapter Five point out that many methods have been used to teach problem solving and that all seem to give positive results. The methods described by various authors work because they focus attention on the definition and development of problem-solving skills and on the devising of activities that give students the intelligent practice that helps them to acquire these skills. Everybody knows the name of the game, they are taught the rules, they are shown some of the moves, and they learn to keep score. The players are not heavily penalized for mistakes, and they can evaluate their own performance.

I have tried to apply some of these ideas in my own teaching. The method that I have used is patterned after the Thinking Aloud Pair Problem Solving (TAPPS) process described by Lochhead and Whimbey in Chapter Five. It works for most people, although not for all. The fact that the problem solver has to speak his or her thoughts aloud is a powerful aid in clarifying those thoughts. When one is musing quietly about something, one's thoughts can be rather woolly, and random thoughts about other matters can intrude. However, when one speaks one's thoughts aloud, one is obliged to organize and structure one's comments so they make sense to the listener. The act of imposing structure on the communication quite literally makes the problem solver think hard about what he or she is saying. (If there is no listener, writing down one's reasoning can have the same effect.) Moreover, although we can "think" at a rate equivalent to 800 to 1,000 words per minute, we can talk at only around 125 to 150 words per minute. Being obliged to talk about what we are thinking forces us to slow down, so that careless errors and errors in logic become less likely to occur.

An example that should be familiar to many readers may serve to underscore the importance of thinking aloud. Most teachers have had a student pop into the office for a little help. "I can't figure out how to do problem 3," she says. "What have you done so far?" you ask. The student proceeds to tell you what she has tried to do. Suddenly, she gets a funny look in her eyes, says "Oh!" and breaks into a smile. "I see," she says, "Thank you very much!" and she goes happily on her way. You appreciate the big thank you, but you wonder what you did. What you did was force the student to talk, talking forced her to make sense, and having to make sense made her able to see how to deal with whatever was puzzling her. It is far better to allow students to figure things out for themselves than it is to show them or tell them. A good tutor asks questions instead of giving answers.

How might you use TAPPS in your teaching? I shall tell what I have done, and you can develop variations of your own. First, I teach the students Polya's strategy. Then, I explain the pairs problem-solving process, divide the class into pairs, and give them a problem to solve. The first problem has nothing to do with the topic of the course, it requires no mathematics and no knowledge of particular facts for its solution, and it is not one that they are likely to have seen before. Whimbey and Lochhead's two books on problem solving and paperbacks from the Dover

Publishing Company series on mathematical and word recreations are rich sources for such problems. The students spend around ten minutes working on the problem, after which it is critiqued by class members. If things are kept moving, all this can be accomplished in one fifty-minute class period.

The students are assigned similar problems for homework, which they are encouraged to solve in pairs. More problems are solved together in class during the next two class periods. Emphasis is placed on following Polya's strategy in approaching the problems and on learning the roles of problem solver and listener. It is important for students to learn these roles and to play their parts honestly.

After this introductory week, the class periods follow the format of most other courses. I present the material, encourage students to ask questions that give me clues about areas where clarification is necessary, and derive equations—a pretty traditional lecture. However, at those times when in the past I would have worked an example problem, I allow students to solve it themselves, working in pairs. A situation is presented, and they follow Polya's strategy to help them arrive at a resolution. It is interesting that all students participate; no one reads the campus newspaper, or prepares for some other class, or sleeps. I think that everyone participates because everyone gets a chance to participate actively, which is a novel experience for many of them, unfortunately. When the solution is critiqued, everyone pays close attention. The satisfaction of those who arrived at an acceptable solution is evident. The rest are interested in finding out where they jumped the track. I do not collect the work to check it or to check up on the students. They already know how they did. I find out about misunderstandings immediately, and I can provide clarification on the spot. One such problem takes fifteen to twenty minutes of class time from start to finish, and I provide such exercises in perhaps a third of the class periods during the semester. I could present the problem and its solution easily in half the time that TAPPS takes, and I could use the time thus saved to cover more of the things that they ought to know about. However, they are learning something now that they were not learning before, and that something is probably more important than any additional content that I might convey. Someone defined education as that which remains when the facts have been forgotten. Once analytical skills have been learned, they stick with us, and it is likely that they will always be in vogue.

Most contributors to this sourcebook have written about work done to improve the methods that can be used to teach problem solving. In Chapter Three, Mary McCaulley writes about the relationship between personality type (in the Jungian sense) and problem-solving style. As she points out, personality type depends on how one takes in information and how one makes decisions. This clearly has important implications both for the way in which we approach problems and for the kinds of problems that we like to solve. Teachers need to keep in mind that there are sixteen different personality types and that the various types have different perceptions, value different things, and differ in their strengths. A knowledge of these differences is valuable when one is dealing with people, particularly when one is working to help them to learn.

Research in individual learning styles also is progressing. The work of David Kolb at Harvard seems particularly productive. His Learning Style Inventory is a brief, forced-choice instrument by which subjects report that they are an accommodator, a diverger, an assimilator, or a converger. These four categories have correlations with the kinds of vocations in which people may be happy, with the areas in which they have strengths and the areas in which they have weaknesses, and with the ways in which they learn best. Kolb's theory says that people learn through feeling (concrete experience, CE), watching (reflective observation, RO), thinking (abstract conceptualization, AC), and doing (active experimentation, AE). In his view, immediate concrete experience forms the basis for observation and reflection. These observations are assimilated into concepts from which new implications for action can be deduced. These implications then serve as guides for the creation of new experiences and so on.

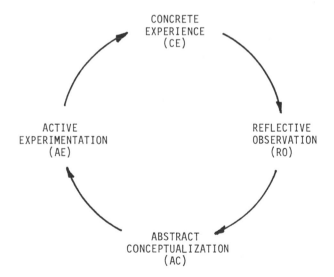

I happen to be a converger. In fact, I am pretty strongly convergent. This implies that I am heavy on AC and AE, and that it is good for tasks that require those attributes. Convergers like the practical application of ideas, they do well on conventional tests, they use hypothetical-deductive reasoning, and they are often found in engineering and the physical sciences. They also are prone to solve the wrong problem and to make decisions too soon. I have very low scores on CE and RO, and that checks, too. Such people often do not complete their work on time, and they find it hard to generate ideas. I do not know David Kolb nor does he know me, but he sure has my number.

Some studies of learning retention indicate that 20 percent is retained if only AC is used, that 50 percent is retained if both AC and RO are used, that 70 percent is retained if AC, RO, and CE are used, and that 90 percent is retained if all four are used. It seems likely that a teacher could improve students' learning if he or she devised instructional activities that included all four learning styles. This should apply to the learning of problem-solving skills, too, I think, and in fact Polya's problem-solving strategy incorporates all four styles. The Define step seems to include CE, RO, and AC, as does the Think About It step. Plan is AC and AE, and Carry Out the Plan is AE. The Look Back step causes the learner to retrace his thoughts from AE back around to CE.

I am not wise enough to see all the ramifications of a general use of the Myers-Briggs Type Indicator or the Learning Style Inventory in higher education, but I am convinced that application of these instruments can be of great help to anyone who truly wants to help students learn. If we understood more about the preferences and the strengths both of our students and of ourselves, it seems that we might be able to make learning and teaching both more effective and more satisfying. Of course, much remains to be learned, but some bright, inquisitive, and creative people have made a good start on mapping the terrain.

Many publications like this one contain extensive lists of references to enable the interested reader to locate nearly everything there is to know about the topic and related areas. These long lists often intimidate me. Further, the authors of the chapters in this sourcebook have already included references for the topics that they address. Accordingly, I shall limit myself here to the resources that I personally have found useful. I shall add comments that might help you to decide whether you want to use them. Art Whimbey and Jack Lochhead have spent a lot of time thinking about the best ways of teaching problem solving. They have written several books, of which I have two:

> *Problem Solving and Comprehension: A Short Course in Analytical Reasoning.* (3rd ed.) Philadelphia: Franklin Institute Press, 1982.
> *Beyond Problem Solving and Comprehension.* Philadelphia: Franklin Institute Press, 1984.

I use these books often—when I can get them back from the people who have borrowed them. They explain how the reader can improve his or her analytical reasoning skills. The first book is easy to read and includes worked examples and about 200 problems of gradually increasing complexity to test the reader's mettle. Answers to the problems are provided. The second book continues in the same vein and provides about 220 additional problems (with answers), some of which require really careful thinking. It also presents student protocols for the solving of problems like the ones they have included in this sourcebook. I recommend both books for students from the freshman year of high school through graduate school. The problems are clever and well thought out. (Note: Franklin Institute Press books are now distributed by Lawrence Erlbaum.)

Moshe Rubinstein, a civil engineer and former head of the systems engineering department at UCLA has written several books on problem solving. Two are especially useful:

Patterns of Problem Solving. Englewood Cliffs, N.J.: Prentice-Hall, 1975.
Tools for Thinking and Problem Solving. Englewood Cliffs, N.J.: Prentice-Hall, 1986.

The first book was developed for Rubinstein's course of the same name at UCLA. It develops a general foundation for problem solving and discusses computers, probability, and five problem-solving models. The second book expands on the ideas set forth in Chapter Two of this sourcebook. Both books require a fair amount of mathematical sophistication.

Donald R. Woods has written a number of articles. The key publications are referenced in his chapter. He is now at work on a book. Two of his other projects merit mention: *PS Newsletter* is a bimonthly publication containing abstracts of articles and books on problem solving, short essays and reports, discussions of attempts to teach problem-solving skills, and a calendar of upcoming workshops and conferences dealing with the subject. Coverage is worldwide. The cost of a one-year subscription (six issues) is $8. To subscribe, send a check or money order to Donald R. Woods, Department of Chemical Engineering, McMaster University, Hamilton, Ontario, Canada L8S 4L7. Woods is also the author of "PS Corner," a lively column on problem solving that appears in each issue of the *Journal of College Science Teaching.*

Dover Publishing Company publishes out-of-print classics from many fields as well as original publications. One series deals with mathematical puzzles and logic problems. Here are three that I have enjoyed:

Graham, L. A. *Ingenious Mathematical Problems and Methods.* New York: Dover, 1959.
Wylie, C. R., Jr. *One Hundred One Puzzles in Thought & Logic.* New York: Dover, 1957.

Phillips, H. *My Best Puzzles in Logic and Reasoning*. New York: Dover, 1961.

L. A. Graham was the founder of Graham Transmissions, which published a house organ called the *Graham Dial* that circulated to more than 25,000 engineers and production executives. Each issue of the publication contained a "Private Corner of Mathematicians," which presented a problem. The best solution received was featured in a subsequent issue. This book presents 100 of these problems and their complete solutions. The problems are not trivial, and some are truly difficult. Most problems require a working knowledge of high school mathematics. For some, it helps to know some number theory and statistics.

Wylie's little book contains 101 puzzles that require no special knowledge or mathematical training but do require the ability to reason clearly. The problems, which are presented in order of increasing difficulty, allow you to "solve murder mysteries and robberies, see which fishermen are liars, and how a blind man can identify color purely by logic." Good fun.

Hubert Phillips wrote puzzle columns for the London *Daily Telegraph* and the *Evening Standard* under the pen name "Caliban." Here are a hundred of his choicest puzzles, including "Tellham Nuthen," "Yachting at Normouth," and "Moulting Feathers." Answers are provided and explained.

The Myers-Briggs Type Indicator and its applications have generated a sizable body of literature. Three works are particularly good:

Myers, I. B., and Myers, P. B. *Gifts Differing*. Palo Alto, Calif.: Consulting Psychologists Press, 1980.

Lawrence, G. D. *People Types and Tiger Stripes: A Practical Guide to Learning Styles*. (2nd ed.). Gainesville, Fla.: Center for Applications of Psychological Type, 1982.

Myers, I. B., and McCaulley, M. H. *Manual: A Guide to the Development and Use of the Myers-Briggs Type Indicator*. Palo Alto, Calif.: Consulting Psychologists Press, 1985.

The Myers-Briggs question booklets, answer sheets, scoring keys, and report forms are restricted materials. That is, they will not be sold to persons who do not execute a statement of professional qualifications so they can be approved for purchase of psychological instruments. Such approval complies with the professional standards of the American Psychological Association. Consulting Psychologists Press (577 College Avenue, Palo Alto, California 94306) publishes the MBTI, and the materials may be ordered either from it or from the Center for Applications of Psychological Type. The materials can be sent only to qualified individuals, not to agencies, schools, or corporations.

The Center for Applications of Psychological Type (2720 N.W. Sixth Street, Gainesville, Florida 32609) is a public, nonprofit organization for research, training, computer scoring, publications, and other services related to the Myers-Briggs Type Indicator. It houses the Isabel Briggs Myers Memorial Library, the most complete collection of research on the MBTI in existence, and the MBTI Data Bank, which contains more than 250,000 records. The Center provides training and consultation on use of the MBTI.

A book by David Kolb is my last piece of recommended reading:

Kolb, D. A. *Experiential Learning: Experience as the Source of Learning and Development*. Englewood Cliffs, N.J.: Prentice-Hall, 1984.

Materials for administering Kolb's Learning Style Inventory can be obtained from McBer and Company, 137 Newbury Street, Boston, Massachusetts, 02116.

There you are: thirteen references and three sources for materials. Reading even a few of the references will provide you with more than you need to know in order to begin to improve your own problem-solving skills and those of your students.

James E. Stice is T. Brockett Hudson Professor of Chemical Engineering and director of the Center for Teaching Effectiveness at the University of Texas at Austin.

Index

A

Abstract conceptualization (AC), learning style of, 105–106
Academic performance, and problem-solving training, 89–91
Active experimentation (AE), learning style of, 105–106
Allen, R. D., 63, 69
Alverno College, competent skills teaching at, 65
American Association for the Advancement of Science (AAAS), 1
American Psychological Association, 108
American Society for Engineering Education, 96
Analytical reasoning. *See* Problem solving
Anderson, T. L., 68, 69
Animals, problem solving in, 6–7
Arkansas, University of, teaching at, 93–94
Armitage, H., 64, 69
Arnold, J. D., 65, 69
Artificial intelligence: and problem-solving process, 9; and tacit knowledge, 58
Association of American Medical Colleges, 90, 92
AT&T, and artificial intelligence, 9
Attitudes: applying, 48–49; and psychological types, 40–42; use of, in problem solving, 15–16, 26, 45
Australia, teaching in, 68

B

Barrows, H. S., 63, 67, 68, 69
Bauman, R. P., 64, 69
Bjork, R., 28, 35
Black, P. J., 64, 66, 69
Blaylock, B. K., 46, 50, 52
Bleasdale, F., 35
Bloom, B. S., 1, 14, 16, 19, 20, 59, 69, 75, 92, 95, 96, 97, 98, 102

Boud, D., 63, 66, 69
Boulton, W. R., 46, 52
Bransford, J., 27, 35
Briggs, K. C., 38
Broder, L. J., 14, 16, 20, 75, 92, 95, 98
Brown, J. M., 68, 69
Brownell, W. A., 5–6, 20
Bukacek, D., 94–95, 96
Butko, J. A., 21

C

Caillot, M., 59, 69
California, University of, Department of Physics and Group in Science and Mathematics Education at, 18
California at Los Angeles, University of (UCLA), problem-solving course at, 1, 11, 96, 107
Canada: and psychological typology, 38; teaching in, 68
Carmichael, JW, Jr., 90, 92
Center for Applications of Psychological Type, 108–109
Chamberlain, J., 68, 69
Chicago, University of, study of problem solving at, 75, 95
Children, young, problem solving in, 6–7
Claparède, E., 1, 2, 13
Clement, J., 17, 18, 20
Cognitive simulation, problem solving related to, 8–9
Cognitive styles, problem solving related to, 7–8. *See also* Learning styles
Computer, and problem-solving process, 8–9, 25
Concrete experience (CE), learning style of, 105–106
Consulting Psychologists Press, 38, 108
Context effects, for information processing, 28
Craik, F., 26, 35
Critical thinking. *See* Problem solving
Crowe, C. M., 70

D

deBono, E., 63, 69
Decision making. *See* Judgment
Dewey, J., 10, 20, 75, 92
Doherty, A., 65, 70
Doig, I. D., 21
Donovan, M. P., 63, 69
Dover Publishing Company, 103-104, 107-108

E

Educational Testing Service, 38
Eich, J., 28, 35
Einstein, A., 13, 28
Eliot, G., 49, 52
Extraversion: applying, 48-49, 51, 52; as attitude, 40-41; in matrix, 42-44; in problem solving, 45; and students and fields, 46

F

Feeling: applying, 48, 49, 50, 51, 52; and judgment and perception, 41; in matrix, 42-44; as mental power, 39-40; in problem solving, 40, 44-45; and students and fields, 46-47
Feuerstein, R., 63, 69
Fields of study, and psychological types, 46-47
Firstenberg, I. R., 1, 23, 36
Fisher, R., 26, 35
Flesch, R., 30, 35
Florida, University of: psychological typology laboratory at, 38; teaching at, 68
Florida Future Scientists, as intuitive, 46
Flower, L., 13, 20
Franks, J., 27, 35

G

Gardiner, J., 28, 35
Gardner, H., 7, 20
Gilhooly, K. J., 6, 8-9, 20
Glenberg, A., 35
Godleski, E. S., 8, 21, 53, 70
Goldstein, I., 9, 21
Good, R., 58, 70

Graham, L. A., 94, 98, 107-108
Gray, T.G.F., 66, 69
Grayson, L., 96
Greenfield, L. B., 1, 5, 22, 96, 102
Griffith University, teaching at, 68
Guided Design, 96

H

Hammurabi, 31
Harrisberger, L., 50, 53, 63, 69, 70
Hayes, J. R., 74, 92
Heller, J. I., 73, 92
Hoffman, T. W., 21, 70
Hough, G. P., Jr., 63, 70
Hoy, F., 46, 52
Huck, S. W., 63, 69
Hunter, J., 90, 92

I

Information: acquisition and retrieval of, 26-29; active processing and retrieval of, 27-28; context effects for processing, 28; and memory monitor, 28-29; problem solving related to processing of, 8-9; structure of, 27, 56, 66. *See also* Perception
Introversion (I): applying, 49, 51; as attitude, 40-41; in matrix, 42-44; in problem solving, 45; and students and fields, 46
Intuition (N): applying, 48, 49, 50, 51, 52; and judgment and perception, 41; in matrix, 42-44; as mental power, 39; in problem solving, 40, 44-45; and students and fields, 46, 47

J

Japan, and psychological typology, 38
Jones, L., 92
Judgment (J): applying, 48, 49, 51, 52; as attitude, 41-42; concept of, 39; in matrix, 42-44; and students and fields, 47; thinking and feeling kinds of, 39-40
Jung, C. G., 2, 7, 37-41, 52, 104

K

Karplus, R., 89, 92
Keller, F. S., 96, 98

Kepner, C. H., 65, 69
Knowledge: base, for problem solving, 23–24; tacit, 56, 58, 66
Knowles, M., 67, 69
Kodatsky, W. F., 58, 66, 71
Kohler, W., 6
Kolb, D., 105–106, 109
Kurlik, S., 58, 69

L

Landauer, T., 28, 35
Landbeck, R., 68, 70
Larkin, J. H., 18–19, 21, 73, 92
Lawrence, G. D., 40, 52, 108
Learning Style Inventory, 105–106, 109
Learning styles, research on, 105–106. *See also* Cognitive styles
Lecture method, and problem solving, 101–102
Leibold, B. G., 11, 21
Lewis, K. G., 97, 99
Lindsay, P., 27, 28, 35
Lochhead, J., 2, 16, 17–18, 19, 21, 64, 67, 70, 73, 75, 84, 85, 89, 90, 92, 96, 99, 102, 103, 106

M

McBer and Company, 109
McCaulley, M. H., 2, 7, 21, 37, 38, 40, 42, 46, 48, 50, 52–53, 59, 70, 104, 108
McKim, R. H., 12, 21
McMaster University, problem-solving course at, 2, 96
Massachusetts, University of: Cognitive Development Group at, 96; Heuristics Laboratory at, 17
Mathematics classes, problem solving in, 84–89
Meiring, S. P., 12, 21, 59, 63, 67, 70
Memory monitor, and information, 28–29
Mental powers: in problem solving, 40; and psychological types, 39–40
Mentkowski, M., 65, 70
Miller, G., 27, 35
Mixed-scanning strategy, for problem solving, 33–34
Montague, W., 27, 35
Morant, E., 90, 92
Moreland, J.L.C., 21

Myers, I. B., 2, 38, 40, 41, 42, 44, 45, 46, 48, 53, 108, 109
Myers, P. B., 40, 53, 108
Myers-Briggs Type Indicator (MBTI): analysis of, 37–53; applications of, 47–50; background on, 37–38; development of, 38; function of, 2, 8, 38, 106; and problem solving, 44–45; and psychological types, 38–44; resources on, 108–109; strategies for using, 44–45; and students and fields, 46–47; and teaching strategies, 51–52

N

Narode, R., 81, 92
National Merit finalists, as intuitive, 46
National Science Foundation, 1
Natter, F. L., 46, 49, 53
Nebraska, University of, ADAPT program of, 96
Nelson-Denny Reading Test, 90
New Jersey, analytical reasoning skills in, 90–91
New Jersey College Basic Skills Placement Test, 90–91
Newton, I., 18
Nippon Recruit Center, and psychological typology, 38
Nisbet, J. A., 46, 53
Norman, D., 27, 28, 35

O

Ohio Department of Education, problem-solving booklets of, 12

P

Penzias, A., 9
Perception (P): applying, 48, 49, 51, 52; as attitude, 41–42; concept of, 39; in matrix, 42–44; in problem solving, 45; sensing and intuitive kinds of, 39; and students and fields, 47
Peters, C. E., 50, 53
Phi Beta Kappas, as intuitive, 46
Phillips, H., 108
Piaget, J., 6–7, 97
Polya, G., 10, 11, 12, 13, 21, 56, 58, 70, 73, 74, 92, 102, 103, 104, 106

Problem: facts on, 29-30; form and content of, 31-32; heuristics for representation of, 29-32; questions on, 31; representations of, 30-31
Problem solving: and academic performance, 89-91; in animals and young children, 6-7; applications of, 7, 8, 9, 11-13, 18-19; applications to teaching of, 47-50; attitudes for, 15-16, 26, 45; awareness of processes of, 66-67; background on, 5-6, 23-25; checklist for, 75-77; cognitive simulation and information processing related to, 8-9; cognitive styles related to, 7-8; conclusions on, 20, 34-35, 101-109; defined, 5-6, 8, 37, 55; expert and novice, 18, 73-74; group, 47-49; heuristics for, 32-34; and implementation, 32-33; information processing for, 26-29; Jungian model for, 37-53; learning, 93-99; in mathematics classes, 84-89; mental powers in, 40; mixed-scanning strategy for, 33-34; necessary features of, 97; and problem representation, 29-32; process of, 13-19; and psychological typology model, 7-8, 44-45, 104-105; rational analysis related to, 9-13; in reading classes, 78-84; resources on, 101-109; skills of, 55-57, 66; steps in, 10-11, 44-45; successful and unsuccessful, 14-16, 75; teaching of, 55-71; with thinking aloud, 13-14, 16-18, 73-92; thinking taught through, 5-22; and tools for thinking, 23-36
Project SOAR (Stress on Analytical Reasoning), 89-90
Psychological types: analysis of model for, 37-53; applications of, 47-50; and attitudes, 40-42; Jung's theory of, 38-44; matrix of, 42-44; and mental powers, 39-40; and problem solving, 7-8, 44-45, 104-105; of students and fields, 46-47; and teaching strategies, 51-52

R

Rational analysis, problem solving related to, 9-13

Raudsepp, E., 63, 70
Reading classes, problem solving in, 78-84
Reed, H. B., 7, 21
Reflective observation (RO), learning style of, 105-106
Reif, F., 18, 21, 73, 92
Resnick, L. B., 75, 92
Ross, D. C., 21
Rubinstein, M. F., 1, 10-11, 21, 23, 26, 35, 36, 96, 99, 107
Ruble, V. E., 53

S

Sanderson, M., 64, 70
Sandler, H. M., 63, 69
Schifter, D., 92
Scholastic Aptitude Test (SAT), 90
Schurr, K. T., 53
Scott, D., 96
Sensing (S): applying, 48, 49, 50, 51, 52; and judgment and perception, 41; in matrix, 42-44; as mental power, 39; in problem solving, 40, 44-45; and students and fields, 46, 47
Simon, H., 8-9, 13, 21
Skinner, B. F., 7
Sloan, E. D., 53, 70
Smith, M. U., 58, 70
Smith, P., 67, 70
Smith, S., 28, 35
Sony Corporation, and implementation, 32-33
Sparks, R. E., 65, 70
Stager, R., 96, 99
Stevens, S. S., 7, 21
Stice, J. E., 3, 16, 17, 21, 67, 70, 93-96, 99, 101, 109
Stonewater, J. K., 11-12, 21, 97, 99
Students, and psychological types, 46-47
Sullivan, V., 9, 21
Swartman, R. K., 21

T

Tamblyn, R. M., 63, 67, 68, 69
Task Force on Thinking, 90
Taylor, P. T., 70
Teaching of problem solving: and academic performance, 89-91; analysis of, 55-71; applications to,

65-68; background on, 55-56; component approach to, 62-65; holistic approach to, 61-63; knowledge about, 58-60; options in, 60-65, 67-68, 97-98, 102-103; summary on, 68-69
Texas, University of, teaching at, 97
Thinking (T): aloud, in problem solving, 13-14, 16-18, 73-92; applying, 48, 49, 50, 51, 52; concepts of, 73-74; judgment and perception in, 41; learning, 93-99; in matrix, 42-44; as mental power, 39; in problem solving, 40, 44-45; reflective, 10, 75; and students and fields, 46-47; teaching, through problem solving, 5-22; tools for, 23-36
Thinking Aloud Pair Problem Solving (TAPPS): and academic performance, 89-91; analysis of, 73-92; background on, 73-75; in mathematics classes, 84-89; method of, 75-78, 103-104; in reading classes, 78-84; summary on, 91. *See also* Whimbey pairs technique
Thomas, G. B., Jr., 81, 92
Tolman, E. C., 6, 21
Tregoe, B. B., 65, 69
Tuchman, B. W., 49, 53

U

Ulesky, A., 90, 92

V

Vincent, H., 92

W

Wales, C. E., 96, 99
Ware, J. R., 46, 53
Weeks, V., 68, 70
Wertheimer, M., 13, 21
West Virginia University, Guided Design at, 96
Whimbey, A., 2, 16, 17, 19, 21, 64, 67, 70, 73, 75, 78, 79, 80, 84, 85, 89, 90, 92, 96, 99, 102, 103, 106
Whimbey Analytical Skills Inventory (WASI), 90-91
Whimbey pairs technique, 2, 17, 67, 68, 73-92, 96. *See also* Thinking Aloud Pair Problem Solving
Wickelgren, W. A., 13, 21
Wood, P. E., 70
Woods, D. R., 2, 11, 16, 17, 21, 55, 58, 59, 66, 67, 70-71, 96, 99, 102, 107
Woodward, P. J., 97, 99
Woodworth, R. S., 6, 13, 21
Wright, J. D., 21, 70
Writing, and problem solving, 12-13
Wylie, C. R., Jr., 107-108

X

Xavier University, Project SOAR at, 89-90

Y

Yokomoto, C. F., 46, 53, 70
Young, R. E., 1, 3

Please remember that this is a library book,
and that it belongs only temporarily to each
person who uses it. Be considerate. Do
not write in this, or any, library book.